D1423938

THE DAILY OFFICE

*Also published by the Joint Liturgical Group
and edited by Ronald C. D. Jasper*

The Renewal of Worship: A book of essays (O.U.P.)
The Calendar and Lectionary: A reconsideration (O.U.P.)

THE DAILY OFFICE

by the Joint Liturgical Group

EDITED BY RONALD C. D. JASPER

LONDON
S.P.C.K. AND THE EPWORTH PRESS
1969

First published in 1968
Reprinted in 1968, 1969
by S.P.C.K.
Holy Trinity Church
Marylebone Road
London, N.W.1
and
The Epworth Press
25/35 City Road
London, E.C.1

Made and printed in Great Britain by
William Clowes and Sons, Limited
London and Beccles

© The Joint Liturgical Group, 1968

SBN 281 02289 5 (S.P C.K.)
7162 0033 3 (Epworth)

CONTENTS

ACKNOWLEDGEMENTS

Quotations from the *Revised Standard Version* of the Bible, copyrighted 1946 and 1952 by the Division of Christian Education of the National Council of the Churches of Christ in the United States of America are used by permission.

The Book of Common Prayer is Crown copyright; extracts used herein are by permission.

Material from *The Prayer Book as proposed in 1928* is reproduced here by permission of the Central Board of Finance of the Church of England.

Material from the *Revised Psalter*, copyrighted 1964, and from *Alternative Services, Second Series: Holy Communion*, copyrighted 1966, 1967 and *Morning and Evening Prayer*, copyrighted 1968 by the Registrars of the Convocations of Canterbury and York, are used by permission.

Thanks are due also to the following for permission to quote from copyright sources:

Cambridge University Press: three collects from the *Scottish Prayer Book*.

A. R. Mowbray & Co. Ltd: one collect from the *Prayer Manual*, by F. B. Macnutt.

Oxford University Press: one collect from *A Book of Public Worship* (compiled by John Huxtable, John Marsh, Romilly Micklem, and James Todd).

The Synod of the Church of South India; seven collects from *The Book of Common Worship of the Church of South India*.

MEMBERS OF THE JOINT
LITURGICAL GROUP

1. **Church of England**
   The Dean of Bristol (The Very Reverend D. E. W. Harrison, M.A.), *Chairman*
   The Right Reverend H. de Candole, M.A. (sometime Bishop of Knaresborough)
   The Reverend Canon R. C. D. Jasper, M.A., D.D., F.R.Hist.S., *Secretary*

2. **Church of Scotland**
   The Reverend R. S. Louden, D.D.
   F. N. Davidson Kelly Esq., LL.B., S.S.C.

3. **The Baptist Union of Great Britain and Ireland**
   The Reverend Neville Clark, M.A., S.T.M.
   The Reverend Stephen F. Winward, M.A., B.D.

4. **The Congregational Church in England and Wales**
   The Reverend J. M. Todd, M.A.
   The Reverend W. E. Evans, B.A., B.D.

5. **The Episcopal Church of Scotland**
   The Bishop of Glasgow, Primus (The Most Reverend F. H. Moncrieff, M.A.)
   The Reverend Canon A. O. Barkway, M.A.

6. **The Methodist Church**
   The Reverend G. S. Wakefield, M.A., B.Litt.
   The Reverend A. Raymond George, M.A., B.D.

7. **The Presbyterian Church of England**
   The Reverend R. Aled Davies, M.A.
   The Reverend W. N. Leak, M.A.

8. **The Churches of Christ**
   The Reverend W. G. Baker, M.A., S.T.M., D.D.

9. **Observer of the Church of Rome**
   The Reverend Canon R. Pilkington

STATEMENT OF 11 OCTOBER 1963

Informal discussions on liturgical matters between interested people from various Churches in Great Britain have indicated that the time is now ripe for the creation of a Joint Liturgical Group which can develop given projects and questions of public worship. The Archbishop of Canterbury was asked to help bring such a Group into being by issuing invitations to the Churches concerned to appoint members. His Grace kindly agreed to do so and himself appointed the representatives of the Church of England, while those of other Churches have been appointed by their respective bodies.

At its first meeting on 10–11 October 1963 the Group elected the Dean of Bristol as its Chairman and Dr Jasper as its Secretary.

It is clearly to be understood that any work produced by this Group will have no authority greater than that which its own members give to it by their own weight; but it will be for particular Churches, through their own customary modes of decision, to make use of the results if they are willing to do so.

The initial projects which the Group has decided to discuss are these:

1. The planning of a Calendar, Forms of Daily Service, and a Lectionary which the Churches might be glad to have in common.

2. The planning of joint forms of service which might be used with the approval of the several Churches on occasions for united worship, such as the Week of Prayer for Unity and Holy Week.

3. The consideration of the structure of the service of Holy Communion.

INTRODUCTION

When the Joint Liturgical Group first met in 1963, it agreed un-animously that the production of a Daily Office would meet a need long felt by a significant number of Free Church ministers; and that if this were approved by the Churches its use would greatly contri-bute to the cause of Christian unity. The Anglican members, more-over, were aware that especially among the younger clergy and in theological colleges a radical revision of the existing office would be welcomed. It was also envisaged that such an office could provide an outline form of prayer and a lectionary which might well be used every day by the laity and, with official encouragement, strengthen the habit of regular Bible reading. The proposed office is therefore intentionally "open-ended", so that it can lead into private prayer and meditation.

The Group also agreed that, if its work was to be acceptable to Anglicans, it must embody traditional elements of the daily offices; while Free Churchmen would also want to see provision made for the use of hymnody.

It is hoped that the following proposals will contain something worthy of consideration and experiment.

D. E. W. HARRISON
Chairman

THE DAILY OFFICE

S. F. WINWARD

What is the office and what is it for? Do Christians need it in any form in the contemporary world? In answering these questions, attention may be drawn at the outset to the three traditional ways in which Christians have offered worship to God. They are public worship, private prayer, and the office. While no hard and fast line can be drawn between them, each of these three ways of prayer has its own basic characteristics and values. Christians of all traditions are familiar with congregational worship and personal prayer. In every place the faithful assemble on the Lord's Day and at other times, to hear God's Word read and preached, to offer to him praise and prayer, and to commemorate with thanksgiving the sacrifice of Christ in the Holy Communion of his body and blood. Dispersed in the world, Christians also have fellowship and hold conservation with God in what is now commonly known as "private prayer". If understood in the sense "strictly private" that phrase is misleading, for no Christian is ever alone at prayer. "When you pray, go into your room and shut the door and pray to your Father who is in secret" (Matt. 6.6). The disciple who obeys that dominical injunction still prays as a member of the Body of Christ, and addresses God as "*Our* Father". Only in the physical sense is the Christian alone at prayer. That, however, is not the distinctive characteristic of private prayer, for in that sense the Christian is sometimes, and indeed nowadays usually, alone when reciting the office. By the phrase "private prayer" reference is made to that aspect of the spiritual life which, because of the uniqueness of each person, necessarily and rightly varies considerably from one to another. In devotion of this kind individuality is at a premium. In private prayer personal characteristics, temperament, gifts, and circumstances are engaged and utilized in the reception of God's Word through reading and meditation and in the offering of praise and prayer. Committed Christians believe that corporate worship (Word and Sacrament) and private prayer are both necessary if we are to offer to the Lord the glory due to his name, and receive the inspiration, nourishment, and strength necessary for continuance and growth in the Christian life. But is any third activity required; is the use of an office either necessary or desirable?

It must be accepted that within certain traditions, especially where great stress has been laid on spontaneity in prayer, a certain suspicion of, and even hostility against, prescribed offices is still to be found. They are associated with the formal and the mechanical, and may even be regarded as the initial stages of a process which, if carried through to its logical conclusion, would end up with something like the Tibetan prayer-wheel! For some, the word "office" has an ancient or a medieval connotation; it conjures up pictures of monks or clerics, of the "churchy" or the other-worldly. These suspicions and misunderstandings can be dispelled only as the nature and purpose of the office is understood. The threefold nature of the office will first be described; we shall then go on to indicate how these three characteristics answer the need of Christians in the contemporary world.

PRAYING WITH THE CHURCH

The office is corporate. It is a means by which Christians join in the perpetual worship offered by Christ with and through the members of his Body, to the eternal Father. Our Lord Jesus Christ "holds his priesthood permanently, because he continues for ever. Consequently he is able for all time to save those who draw near to God through him, since he always lives to make intercession for them" (Heb. 7. 24-5). This prayer which our exalted High Priest offers perpetually to the Father, he offers with and through the members of the Body of which he is the Head. That Body is the Church militant on earth, triumphant in heaven. In the Book of Revelation, John of Patmos describes the worship of heaven by means of symbols taken in part from the worship of the churches of his own time and place. Every creature in the universe—heaven, earth, sea, underworld—joins in the doxology of praise to God the Creator and Christ the Redeemer. The worship is perpetual and unanimous;

"the four living creatures" representing the whole animate creation "never cease to sing", and the myriads of angels and of the
redeemed praise and pray with one voice. The heavenly worship
is concerted, common, unceasing (Rev. 4 and 5). The worship
offered up by the Church militant here on earth is also unceasing.
The prayers of a Christian and the services of a church in a particular place begin and end. The worship of the Church universal,
even here on earth, never begins or ends.

> As o'er each continent and island
> The dawn leads on another day,
> The voice of prayer is never silent,
> Nor dies the strain of praise away.[1]

When Christians assemble in a particular place for divine service,
for Word and Sacrament, they join in this perpetual worship of the
Church triumphant (and some would add—expectant) and militant. It is "with angels and archangels and all the company of
heaven" and with all the faithful on earth, that we offer adoration
and thanksgiving to the Lord of hosts. Now the office may be described as a way of doing this when the local church is not assembled
for the divine service of Word and Sacrament. The analogy of
broadcasting has frequently been used. When the radio or the tele-
vision is switched on in a particular home, there is a "tuning in"
to a transmission which was in process before listening or viewing
began, and which will continue after the set has been switched off.
By means of this instrument, the office, we tune in to the common,
concerted, perpetual worship of the Body of Christ. That worship
is being offered before we join in, and it will continue to be offered
when we fall out. To say the office is to contribute our little quota of
devotion to the unceasing offering of praise and prayer which as-
cends from the whole Church through Christ to the Father.

The office should be recited with the intention of joining in the
common prayer of the Church. Whether it is said by a Christian
alone, or by a group of Christians met for the purpose, it is to be
offered "with all God's people" (Eph. 3.18, N.E.B.). Much of the
language of the office, especially the use of "we" rather than "I"

---

[1] From the hymn, *The day thou gavest*, by John Ellerton

15

is itself a reminder of its corporate nature. Even when the pronoun "I" is used, as frequently in the Psalter, its representational character should be kept in mind. The psalmist speaks for the larger group to which he belongs. The occasional transition in the same psalm from "I" to "we", from the one to the many (or in the reverse direction), is indicative of the fact that the people of God, Israel, is speaking through the Davidic king or through the psalmist. It is in accordance with the corporate nature of the office that the basic material used in it should be taken from that which all Christians have in common—the holy Scriptures. For from the beginning the edifice of the divine office has rested upon two pillars: the reading of the Scriptures and the recitation of the Psalter in orderly fashion. It is by the systematic and habitual use of this common material that we both hear the Word of God and address to him our praises and prayers together with all his people.

THEOCENTRIC PRAISE

The office is objective. It is theocentric. Its primary purpose is to offer praise to the "one God and Father of us all, who is above all and through all and in all" (Eph. 4.6). The Shorter Catechism compiled by the Westminster Assembly in 1647 opens with the well-known Question and Answer. "What is the chief end of man?": "Man's chief end is to glorify God and to enjoy him for ever". The office is a means to the realization of that end—the offering up of disinterested praise to the transcendent God. For this reason also, the basis of the office is the orderly reading of the Scriptures and the recitation of psalms. The Scriptures are the record of the revelation of God in the history of Israel and in the life, death, and resurrection of Jesus Christ. They are the written testimony of prophets and apostles to the "wonderful deeds" of him who called us out of darkness into his marvellous light (1 Pet. 2.9). To read the Scriptures is to recite the acts of God, and to set the mind on him to whom all worship should be directed. Through the Bible "wherein are the living oracles of God", he reveals to us his mind and purpose. "In the Christian order of salvation it is of primary importance to realize always that God is speaking to us, that God's grace is calling us. Then, and only then, can we turn to God with our

16

response".[1] In the Book of Psalms, itself part of Scripture, there is both revelation and response. To the revelation of God, whether in creation or in history, whether in Temple worship or in the experience of the individual, the psalmists respond with praise and prayer. While containing prayer of every kind, the dominant theme of the Psalter as a whole is the joyous praise of God. And so, in the office, through the recital of Scripture and psalm, we unite with all God's people to "give to him glorious praise" (Ps. 66.2). To give *to him*. There is no doubt that many and great benefits are received by those who pray the office habitually, and with some of these we shall be concerned presently. But they are the indirect results, the inevitable by-products. The primary purpose of the office is disinterested and objective. In one Spirit we have access through Christ to the Father (Eph. 2.18), that we may give to him the glory due to his name.

THE PRIMACY OF THE WILL

The office is volitional. It has to do primarily with the will. The word "office", from the Latin *officium*, means a duty or service required. At this point the modern usages of the word are helpful. Nowadays, an office is either a position in a society with duties attached to it, or it is a place for transacting business. It carries the connotation of duty, responsibility, work, business. The recitation of the office, which by St Benedict was called the "work of God," is primarily a matter of obligation. It is based upon the primacy of the will in worship, the steadfast intention to offer praise to God. Along with corporate worship and private prayer, it is part of the *regula*—the "disciplined response to the love of God, crystallized into a system out of the living experience of the organic Church".[2] In this connection, it is important that we should recover the full biblical meaning of the word "heart". For the Hebrews, the heart "was the innermost spring of individual life, the ultimate source of all its physical, intellectual, emotional, and volitional energies, and consequently the part of man through which he normally achieved

---

[1] Joseph A. Jungmann, *The Early Liturgy* (Indiana 1959; English edn, 1960), p. 284.

[2] Martin Thornton, *The Rock and the River* (London 1965), p. 27.

contact with the divine".[1] Although all the emotions may be attributed to it, contrary to the modern connotation of the word the emphasis in the Bible is upon the heart as the centre of intellectual life and especially of the will. "You shall love the Lord your God with all your heart, and with all your soul, and with all your mind, and with all your strength" (Mark 12.30). Every aspect of the personality should be involved and engaged in the offering of worship to God. Emotion, thought, and will should combine to provide the material for the spiritual sacrifice. There is a widespread tendency, however, to identify the heart with the feelings, and thus to mistake the part for the whole. This may lead to an over-stress on spontaneity, and to the assumption that a man cannot pray acceptably unless his feelings are stirred, his affections kindled. Yet the responsible citizen discharges the duties of his office and the trustworthy worker goes to the office whether he feels like it or not. To worship God is an obligation to be discharged irrespective of the presence or absence of feeling. The office is the embodiment of this intention, this determination to praise and pray with disciplined regularity.

FELLOWSHIP IN PRAYER

There are many members of the Church today, both ministerial and lay, who have spoken of their need of the office type of prayer. Left to themselves without the aid of a stable practice some, finding the path of prayer too difficult to tread, have abandoned it altogether. Others have retained the practice of private prayer and rightly appreciate and value the tradition of spontaneity. They are nevertheless conscious that their private prayers need to be complemented (not replaced) by the use of a method which will enable them with the whole Church to offer disinterested praise and prayer to God with disciplined regularity. The various ways in which the recitation of the office can help us today may be indicated by taking up in turn the three key words: corporate, objective, volitional.

There are many situations today in which Christians have to live, work, and pray, in some cases for long periods of time, without the

[1] R. C. Denton, *The Interpreter's Dictionary of the Bible* (Abingdon Press, Nashville 1962), Vol. II, p. 549.

inspiration and support of congregational worship and Christian fellowship. The layman, isolated at work, and perhaps also at home, is subject to the insidious influence of apathy and unbelief. The missionary, set down in a remote outpost overseas, or the minister on a new housing estate in Britain may, because isolated from his true environment, feel "like a pelican of the wilderness" (Ps. 102.6). To all such, the office can be of great value. For by this means, to put it paradoxically, the Christian can pray with the Church when the Church is not present. Reciting scriptures, psalms, canticles, collects, prayers, he is using the same words which thousands have said, are saying, and will say. He joins with all God's people in the chorus of praise. "I'm fed up with this ghastly picture of prayer as a private telephone line with or without a voice at the other end. It's much more like you and me playing our second fiddles in an unending heavenly orchestral symphony of praise and joy. When we pray, we take up our fiddles, and when we stop we put them down again—but the music never stops".[1] This deliverance from isolation into concerted activity may be realized even more fully where Christians gather to recite the office. The bodily presence of others does not make the office more corporate; yet whenever the Body of Christ becomes visible, audible, tangible, we, in our frailty, are thereby helped to realize the communal nature of our worship. Since part of the meaning of salvation is to be delivered from isolation into the common life of the Body of Christ, the office itself can be a means of grace, an instrument used by the Spirit of God for our sanctification.

OBJECTIVITY IN PRAYER

"Could you, only for a moment, fix your mind on something not yourself?"[2] This appeal made by a heavenly spirit to a soul in danger of final perdition may serve as a challenge to us. For the sin of self-centredness may corrupt even our prayers. "God bless me and my wife; my son John and his wife; us four, no more, Amen."[3] A small circle with oneself at the centre may be substituted for "the

[1] Basil Moss, *Spirituality for Today*, ed. Eric James (London 1967), p. 161.

[2] C. S. Lewis, *The Great Divorce* (London 1946), p. 57.

[3] Quoted by L. H. Marshall in *The Challenge of New Testament Ethics* (London 1946), p. 141.

whole family in heaven and on earth" (Eph. 3.15, N.E.B. margin) with the Father at the centre. His own needs narrowly conceived, or even his own wants, and not God's glory, may become the chief end of man. We do indeed need God, and have been taught by Christ to bring all our needs to him. In the prayers of this office, and especially in the "open-ended" prayers, the needs of others and our own personal needs have a rightful place. That, however, should not be the first place. The Lord's Prayer was given to us as a pattern for all our praying—"pray then like this" (Matt. 6.9). We are taught to put God first, to give him the supreme place, to desire his glory, kingdom, and will above all things. The adoration of God is followed by the petitions concerned with human need, which are thus set in true perspective. We have been created, redeemed, and sanctified to adore and to obey God. Because the office is theocentric, it is a powerful aid and stimulus to the offering up of disinterested praise. Created and reformed by the Spirit through the Church, it may be used to deliver us from undue subjectivity, and to enable us to join with all God's people in objective praise. The purpose of the office has been achieved when we are truly able to say, "We give thanks to thee for thy great glory, O Lord God, heavenly King, God the Father Almighty."

REGULARITY IN PRAYER

When we are babes in Christ and throughout the period of our spiritual adolescence, we are inclined to depend on emotion. God, in his goodness and mercy, provides us from time to time with such pleasant emotional sweetmeats to keep us going along the way of prayer. "But grown men can take solid food" (Heb. 5.14, N.E.B.). God trains us for his service by withdrawing, sometimes for long periods, the uplift, the affective stimulants and rewards, so that we may no longer be raw recruits but disciplined veterans. At all times, like the Saviour with his face steadfastly set to go to Jerusalem, we must will, determine, to give to the Lord the glory due to his name. We can learn to worship him with, without, or against our feelings, as the case may be. We can refuse to build the house of prayer on the sand of feeling; we can build it on the rock of the will, recreated and enabled by the Holy Spirit. By nature our feelings are inconstant. To rely on them is to be "tossed to and fro and carried about by every wind", or, more likely, to be left in the doldrums unable to sail anywhere at all. To rely on mood and inclination is to pray by fits and starts. The Christian should value the presence of emotion in prayer, but never rely upon it. He will continue to seek God even when he is "in a dry and weary land where no water is" (Ps. 63.1). There is evidence that some, brought up to regard feeling and spirituality as synonymous, have succumbed to the temptations which assail almost all Christians during prolonged seasons of weariness and aridity. It is then, most of all, that system, habit, prescribed order, are required. By means of the office we may move on from the spasmodic to the habitual in prayer, and the set of the will (constancy of purpose, regular practice) is itself a costly and precious offering to God.

HOLY WORLDLINESS

The office is a godsend today, because of the speed and pressure of life. For many people there are not enough hours in the day or days in the week. There rarely seems to be enough time to do what has to be done.

And so all men run after time, Lord.
They pass through life running—hurried, jostled, overburdened, frantic and they never get there. They haven't time.
In spite of all their efforts they're still short of time, a great deal of time.
Lord, you must have made a mistake in your calculation.

There is a big mistake somewhere,
The hours are too short,
The days are too short,
Our lives are too short.[1]

In such circumstances the office is invaluable. For some of the traditional forms of private prayer and meditation presuppose that the Christian has at his disposal, or is able, to "set aside" lengthy periods. The recitation of the office, on the other hand, does not take very long. Although the time may be extended indefinitely if desired, not more than fifteen to twenty minutes is necessary. There

[1] Michel Quoist, *Prayers of Life* (Dublin 1965), p. 77.

is something even more important. The busy man who uses the office is saved from the necessity of having to make decisions about everything. Making decisions takes time and energy. The office, with the scriptures to be read, the psalms and prayers to be said, is there all ready to be used.

It is true that the office may appear to be the exact antithesis of the type of spirituality relevant to life in a secular society in the latter half of the twentieth century. Does it not foster "a fugitive and cloistered virtue, unexercised and unbreathed, that never sallies out and sees her adversary, but slinks out of the race, where that immortal garland is to be run for, not without dust and heat?"[1] Does it not encourage escapist, pietistic, other-worldly attitudes? Is it not better to look for God in the "dust and heat"? Surely the spirituality for today may be described by the phrase "holy worldliness". "If one were to try to sum up the marks of this mode, or mood of prayer, certain things recur. Its controlling rubric might be the words of Coventry Patmore, 'You may see the disc of Divinity quite clearly through the smoked glass of humanity, but not otherwise'. Indeed, its key preposition is 'through'. God is to be met in, with, and under, not apart from, response to the world and the neighbour."[2] Those who accept this truth and welcome this emphasis must nevertheless go on to ask the crucial question—how? How is this ideal made real? For most Christians are not habitually aware of the presence of God in inter-personal relationships; they are not habitually conscious of the fact that they are responding to Christ in their dealings with people. How do we become more constantly aware of "the beyond in the midst of life"? Through becoming alive to God in Jesus Christ, through our incorporation into his Body by baptism and faith, through Word and Sacrament, through the practice of private prayer and meditation, through the daily recitation of the office. Habitual recollection is the fruit of life-long discipline; it is the hallmark of Christian maturity. In the creation of this awareness of God, as present at all times and in all places, as confronting us in the demands and opportunities of daily life, as meeting us in our personal relationships, the recitation

[1] John Milton, *Areopagitica*.
[2] John A. T. Robinson, *Exploration into God* (London 1967), p. 127.

of the office can play an important part. Habitual recollection is the end to which the office is one important means. The purpose of saying it at the beginning and at the end of each day is not the consecration of those limited periods of time, but the sanctification of all time. The ultimate purpose of public worship, the office, and private prayer is one and the same.

> So shall no part of day or night,
>   Unblest or common be;
> But all my life, in every step,
>   Be fellowship with thee.[1]

This state of habitual recollection, however, must not be confused with thinking about God. It is certainly not the purpose of devotional discipline to encourage the faithful to try to think about God all the time. A man driving a bus down Oxford Street, London during the "rush hour" ought not to be thinking about God! That is the meaning of Archbishop Temple's challenging dictum: "In order to serve God properly, there are times when we must forget him". That does not mean that there are times when we must cease to worship him. For true worship is not one activity among others; it is synonymous with the whole of a reverent life. When he is not thinking about him at all, a man may acknowledge God's worth in his personal relationships, in his domestic and social life, in his daily work and recreational activities, in the direction and right use of all his powers. Yet this will be so only if there are special times during which he does consciously think of God and deliberately offer to him his life and work. The state of habitual recollection is like a happy marriage. The devoted husband and wife do not spend all, or even most, of their time thinking about each other; yet they remain "in holy estate of matrimony". Wherever they are, whatever they are doing, their whole existence is a "being-in-love". But an abiding relationship of that nature is maintained only because there are times of fully conscious dialogue and communion. The purpose of the daily office is to create and sustain an habitual awareness, an abiding relationship. The ultimate objective is *life* "in Christ".

[1] H. Bonar (*Hymns A & M* 373).

TIME, PLACE, AND METHOD

Something must be said in conclusion in answer to the questions *when*, *where*, and *how*? It is in accordance with both Scripture and tradition, and it is obviously fitting, that worship should be offered to God at the beginning and at the end of each day. The appropriate times for reciting the office cannot be more precisely indicated, for they must needs vary from one person or group to another. It will suffice to suggest that the first part should be said in the morning, and the second part, in the familiar words of an office hymn, "before the ending of the day". Like Aaron and his descendants, who were commanded to burn fragrant incense on the altar every morning, and when the lamps were lit in the evening, so the "royal priesthood" of the new covenant, at the beginning and ending of each day, should offer to God the incense of praise and prayer (Exod. 30.7–8).

The places where the office is said are likely to be as varied as the times. Clergy and ministers may be able to pray the office in church, whether alone or with others, and students may use the college chapel. For most of us today, the place is more likely to be a bedroom, a study, a railway compartment, the top deck of a bus, some spot at work before work begins, a seat in a park, a restaurant, a city church. It is, however, important to be definite about the when and the where, if this offering of worship is to be habitual. It has already been emphasized that the corporate nature of the office in no way depends on the physical presence or absence of others. Yet the custom of saying the office, whenever possible, with others "present in the body", is to be commended. The "two or three . . . gathered" may be the members of a Christian family, the teacher and pupils of a school, the staff and students of a college, the employer and employees at work, the clergy and ministers at fraternal, the pastor and people at a mid-week meeting, the priest and parishioners in church. The psalms and the canticles may be said together throughout, or the leader and the people may say alternate verses. The leader may also arrange beforehand for the Scripture lesson or lessons to be read by someone else. An individual saying the office may well desire to combine it with private prayer, whether in the morning or evening, or on both occasions. Such a combination is facilitated by the form of these offices. The person using them is free to meditate as long as time permits on the scriptures read, and other written or extempore prayers may be added as desired to the "open-ended" prayers provided.

The practice of sitting for the recitation of the psalter and of the scripture lessons, and of kneeling for the prayers, is commended. The office should not only be read but also recited—that is, the words should not only be taken in through the eyes, but also spoken with the lips. When circumstances permit, it is advisable to say it out loud. If this is not possible because of the close proximity of others not sharing in the act, it is still advisable to say the words quietly with the lips, and not only think them in the mind. For the office is a spiritual sacrifice to be offered up to God. As Israel of old offered up animal victims, so we take with us words, we offer "the fruit [literally, the bulls] of our lips" (Hos. 14.2). Joining in the worship of the one fellowship which the Holy Spirit creates and indwells, we offer up our praises and prayers daily, through the one Mediator Jesus Christ, to the one God and Father of us all. "Through him then let us continually offer up a sacrifice of praise to God, that is, the fruit of lips that acknowledge his name" (Heb. 13.15).

THE PROPOSALS

THE STRUCTURE OF THE DAILY OFFICE

MORNING
Sentence or Versicles and Responses
Venite
Psalm
Lessons (a) Old Testament
　　　　(b) Epistle
Silence
Canticle or Hymn
Here may be said The Creed
Lord's Prayer
Collects (a) of the Day
　　　　(b) Morning

. . . .

Here may follow the Intercessions or other prayers

EVENING
Sentence or Versicles and Responses
Psalm
Lesson—Gospel
Silence
Canticle or Hymn
Act of Penitence
Collect—Evening

. . . .

Here may follow the Thanksgivings or other prayers

THE SENTENCES OR
VERSICLES AND RESPONSES

The Office shall begin with *either* a General Sentence *or* a Seasonal Sentence *or* Versicles and Responses.

1. GENERAL SENTENCES

God is spirit, and those who worship him must worship in spirit and truth. *John 4.24*

Seek the Lord while he may be found, call upon him while he is near. *Isaiah 55.6*

In everything by prayer and supplication with thanksgiving let your requests be made known to God. *Philippians 4.6*

Through Christ let us continually offer up a sacrifice of praise to God, that is, the fruit of lips that acknowledge his name. *Hebrews 13.15*

To the only God, our Saviour, through Jesus Christ our Lord, be glory, majesty, dominion, and authority, before all time and now and for ever. Amen. *Jude 25*

2. SEASONAL SENTENCES

9th before Christmas to the end of 5th before Christmas
Our help is in the name of the Lord, who made heaven and earth. *Psalm 124.8*

4th before Christmas (Advent 1) to Christmas
The glory of the Lord shall be revealed, and all flesh shall see it together. *Isaiah 40.5*

Christmas Day to the end of Christmas 1
Unto us a child is born: O come let us adore him. Alleluia! *Isaiah 9.6*

Christmas 2 to the end of Christmas 6
The grace of God has appeared for the salvation of all men. *Titus 2.11*

9th before Easter to the end of 7th before Easter
Jesus said: Come to me, all who labour and are heavy-laden, and I will give you rest. *Matthew 11.28*

29

6th before Easter (Lent 1) to the end of 3rd before Easter
Jesus said: For their sake I consecrate myself, that they also may be consecrated in truth. *John 17.19*

2nd before Easter and Holy Week
Christ the Lord became obedient unto death, even death on a cross.
Philippians 2.8

Easter Week
The Lord has risen indeed. Alleluia! *Luke 24.34*

Easter 1 to Ascension
Blessed be the God and Father of our Lord Jesus Christ! By his great mercy we have been born anew to a living hope through the resurrection of Jesus Christ from the dead. *1 Peter 1.3*

Ascension to Pentecost
Since we have a great high priest over the house of God, let us draw near with a true heart in full assurance of faith. *Hebrews 10.21*

Pentecost to the end of Pentecost 5
Jesus said: You shall receive power when the Holy Spirit has come upon you; and you shall be my witnesses. *Acts 1.8*

Pentecost 6 to the end of Pentecost 10
If anyone is in Christ, he is a new creation; the old has passed away, behold, the new has come. *2 Corinthians 5.17*

Pentecost 11 to the end of Pentecost 16
God was in Christ reconciling the world to himself. *2 Corinthians 5.19*

Pentecost 17 to the end of Pentecost
Jesus said: Lo, I am with you always, to the close of the age.
Matthew 28.20

3. VERSICLES AND RESPONSES

O Lord, open thou our lips;
And our mouth shall show forth thy praise.
O God, make speed to save us;
O Lord, make haste to help us.
Glory be to the Father, and to the Son;
and to the Holy Spirit:
*As it was in the beginning, is now, and ever shall be ;
world without end. Amen.*
Praise ye the Lord;
The Lord's Name be praised.

THE VENITE

While the Group agreed that it was important not to omit the final verses of the Venite, with their references to "today" and to judgement, it nevertheless realized that these verses present a problem to many people. It has therefore followed the practice of the Protestant Episcopal Church in the United States of America, replacing the last four verses with the last verse of Psalm 96. The essential meaning is thus retained, but in simpler language. There is, of course, precedent for joining passages from different psalms to form a single unit within the Psalter itself. The text below is taken from the Revised Psalter.

1 O come let us sing unto the Lord:
   let us heartily rejoice in the Rock of our salvation.
2 Let us come before his presence with thanksgiving:
   and sing loudly unto him with psalms.
3 For the Lord is a great God:
   and a great King above all gods.
4 In his hand are all the deep places of the earth:
   and the heights of the mountains are his also.
5 The sea is his and he made it:
   and his hands prepared the dry land.
6 O come let us worship and bow down:
   and kneel before the Lord our maker.
7 For he is our God, and we are his people and the sheep of his pasture:
   today if ye will hear his voice ye shall know his power.
8 For he cometh to judge the earth:
   in righteousness shall he judge the world, and the peoples in his faithfulness.

Glory be to the Father, and to the Son: and to the Holy Spirit;
As it was in the beginning, is now, and ever shall be world without end.
Amen.

THE TABLE OF PSALMS

The Psalms are a treasury of devotion and have always been essential to the structure of the daily office. For these reasons the Group was convinced that they must still be integral to the Office. Nevertheless, there is a considerable body of evidence which indicates that the provision of long passages from the Psalms does not encourage the regular recitation of the Office. It is now proposed to recite the Psalter four times a year instead of once a month; while the average number of verses at each service is just over thirteen. On no occasion does the total number of verses exceed twenty-five.

The Group knows of no liturgical principle which requires the use of the entire Psalter in public worship. Some passages are unsuitable; some passages are obscure; and other passages appear more than once. Certain psalms and portions of psalms have therefore been omitted; but the omissions have been kept to a minimum.

As far as possible the psalms are recited in their biblical order, while the verse references are those of the RSV. Of the longer historical psalms only portions have been used, but an attempt has been made to retain the devotional lessons which these psalms embody. No psalm is omitted simply because of its length, and where a psalm has been divided an attempt has been made either to use it all on the same day, or to use it at consecutive services. The exception is Psalm 119. It would seem devotionally difficult to use this psalm every morning and evening for a whole week. The Group felt, however, that two sections might be used effectively every Saturday evening, as a summing up of the week's use and reflection on the Word of God.

The original intention was to make the evening portion slightly shorter than the morning portion. The difference in length has, however, finally proved to be very small. But the regular use of the Venite (Psalm 95) in the morning restores the balance originally intended.

1. The following psalms have been omitted as generally unsuitable: 58, 59, 60, 79, 83, 109, 120.

2. Psalm 14 is omitted, being duplicated in Psalm 53; and Psalm 108 is omitted, vv. 1–5 being duplicated in Psalm 57, and vv. 6–13 being both duplicated in Psalm 60 and regarded as unsuitable.
3. Psalm 91 is transposed with Psalm 92, being thought more suitable for evening recitation.
4. If the whole of Psalm 136 is used, the refrain need not be recited in each verse.

		MORNING	EVENING
Week 1	M	1, 2. 1–8	3, 4
	T	5. 1–8,11–12	6. 1–9
	W	7. 1–11,17	8
	T	9. 1–10	10. 1–12,16–18
	F	11. 1–5, 7	12
	S	13, 15	119. 1–16
Week 2	M	16	17
	T	18. 1–16	18.17–31
	W	19	20
	T	21. 1–7,13	23
	F	22. 1–21	22.22–31
	S	24	119.17–32
Week 3	M	25	26
	T	27	28. 1–3, 5–9
	W	29	30
	T	31. 1–8	31. 9–24
	F	32	33
	S	35. 9–18	119.33–48
Week 4	M	34. 1–10	34.11–22
	T	36	37. 1–11
	W	37.12–29	37.30–40
	T	38. 1–9	38.10–22
	F	39	40. 1–10 (or end)
	S	41	119.49–64
Week 5	M	42	43
	T	44. 1–8	45

		MORNING	EVENING
	W	46	47
	T	48	49
	F	50. 1–15	51
	S	52	119.65–80
Week 6	M	53	54
	T	55. 1–8,16–22	56
	W	57	61
	T	62	63. 1–8
	F	64	65
	S	66	119.81–96
Week 7	M	67	70
	T	68. 1–18	68.19–20,24–35
	W	69. 1–13a	69.13b–21,29–36
	T	71. 1–14	71.15–24
	F	73. 1–14	73.15–28
	S	72	119.97–112
Week 8	M	74. 1–12	74.13–23
	T	75. 1–7, 9–10	76
	W	77	78. 1–7
	T	80	81
	F	82	84
	S	85	119.113–28
Week 9	M	86	87
	T	88	90
	W	89. 1–18	89.19–37
	T	92	91
	F	93	94. 1–2,14–23
	S	96	119.129–44
Week 10	M	97	98
	T	99,100	101
	W	102. 1–11	102.12–28
	T	103	105. 1–15
	F	104. 1–23	104.24–35
	S	106. 1–8,43–48	119.145–60

		MORNING	EVENING
Week 11	M	107. 1–16	107.17–32
	T	107.33–43	110,111
	W	112	113
	T	114	115
	F	118. 1–18	118.19–29
	S	116,117	119.161–76
Week 12	M	121	122,123
	T	124,125	126,127
	W	128,129	130,131
	T	132	133,134
	F	135. 1–7,15–21	136. 1–9,23–6 (or all)
	S	137. 1–6	138
Week 13	M	139. 1–18,23–4	140. 1–7,12–13
	T	141. 1–5, 8–10	142
	W	143. 1–11	144
	T	145. 1–7	145. 8–21
	F	146	147
	S	148	149. 1–5,150

THE LECTIONARY

The general plan of this two-year Lectionary is to read the whole of the New Testament once a year and nearly the whole of the Old Testament once every two years. In the Old Testament lections the principle of track reading is employed whereby certain passages of a book might be omitted, but the essential argument or narrative of the book is not impaired. In this way we believe that all the important passages of the Old Testament are read. Only passages of exceptional importance, such as the Servant Songs in the Book of Isaiah, are read in both years. As far as possible books are read through systematically, and only at certain special seasons, such as Holy Week, are passages on successive days chosen from different parts of the Bible. An attempt has also been made to fit the weekday lectionary to the same pattern as the Sunday lectionary. Since the Lectionary is on a two-yearly basis, and each day has readings from Old Testament, Epistles, and Gospels, in churches where it is customary to have a daily Eucharist it would be possible to use Year 1 for the Office and Year 2 for the Eucharist, both in the same year; then in the following year, the two cycles could be transposed.

FIRST YEAR

PRE-CHRISTMAS

In the Old Testament the Lectionary begins, as does the Sunday lectionary, with readings from Genesis. These are followed on the 4th before Christmas (Advent 1), according to tradition, by readings from Isaiah, many of which are eschatological in character, and these continue until the end of the year, with the exception of the 2nd week before Christmas (Advent 3), when Elijah passages from 1 Kings provide the background to Gospel readings on John Baptist.

From 18–31 December there are special lessons, and these will always take precedence over readings for the 2nd week before Christmas. The pre-Christmas period Epistles are concerned with the reading of the book of Revelation, which is again in line with tradition, and helps to emphasize the eschatological element of this season. This is followed by Colossians in the 2nd week before Christmas, which fits well with the Elijah and John Baptist passages, and is followed from 18–31 December by 2 and 3 John, Philemon, and Philippians, in which the readings from chapter 2 fall suitably on Christmas Day. The Gospel readings in this period come from St John, being replaced in the 4th week before Christmas (Advent 1) with eschatological passages from Matthew 23—25. These are followed by John Baptist passages from St Luke and St Matthew in the 2nd week before Christmas, while from 18–31 December come the early chapters of St Matthew and St Luke, the former of which is then continued through the post-Christmas period.

POST-CHRISTMAS

In the Old Testament the readings from Isaiah are continued throughout this period. In the Epistles, Ephesians, the Pastoral Epistles, and 1 John follow—all of which contain christological passages making them suitable for this season, while the Gospels continue the systematic reading of St Matthew.

PRE-EASTER

In the Old Testament Jeremiah is read until the beginning of Holy Week, while in the Epistles, Galatians, James, and Hebrews are read. The Gospels also continue reading through St Matthew, the later chapters of which are appropriate when thoughts turn to Holy Week. Chapter 28 with its resurrection narrative is, however, reserved for Easter Week. In Holy Week and Easter Week there are special readings, many of which have been used during this season in the lectionary of the Church of England.

POST-EASTER

In the Old Testament there is now a systematic reading of historical books beginning with Exodus, and this continues until the middle of Pentecost, broken into by the special readings during the Octave of Pentecost. Similarly, in the Epistles there is a systematic reading of 1 and 2 Peter, 1 and 2 Thessalonians, and then Romans, followed by the reading of Acts during the Pentecost period. In the Gospels, the reading of the resurrection appearances from St Mark, St Luke, and St Matthew are followed by the systematic reading of St Mark, which also continues into Pentecost.

PENTECOST

In the Old Testament special readings are provided for the week-days following Pentecost, after which come selections from Numbers and Deuteronomy about the People of God. These are followed by further selections from Joshua and Judges, and then by Joel, Nahum, Habakkuk, and selections from Job and Chronicles. The last weeks, some of which will not be needed every year, provide selected readings from the Apocrypha, with alternatives from the Old Testament. In the Epistles, Acts is followed appropriately by 1 and 2 Corinthians, Jude, and part of Ephesians. In the Gospels, St Mark is followed by the systematic reading of St Luke, while the last week (not often needed) duplicates passages from the Sermon on the Mount in St Matthew.

SECOND YEAR

PRE-CHRISTMAS

Here again the Old Testament lectionary begins with another set of passages from Genesis, followed by further readings from Isaiah. Eschatological passages from Daniel, Zephaniah, and Zechariah appear in the 3rd week before Christmas; while in the 2nd week before Christmas further Elijah passages appear. Once again Isaiah passages also fill the period 18–31 December. The Epistles cover the systematic reading of Romans, followed by the eschatological themes of 1 and 2 Thessalonians; while in the Gospels, St Mark 1—8 is followed in the Advent period by eschatological passages from St Luke, chapters 17, 19–21, and then John Baptist passages from St Matthew and St Luke. The period 18–31 December is covered by specially selected passages from St John.

POST-CHRISTMAS

The Old Testament readings from Isaiah are followed by Amos, Hosea, and Micah, while the Epistles come from 1 John, 1 Corinthians, and 2 Peter. The Gospels read through St Luke, and these continue until the 6th week before Easter.

PRE-EASTER

In the Old Testament a beginning is made on 1 and 2 Samuel, and this continues, with the exception of Holy Week and Easter Week, with 1 and 2 Kings in the post-Easter period. In the Epistles, 2 Corinthians is followed by Galatians, Colossians, and James; while in the Gospels, St Luke is followed by the second half of St Mark, the first half having been read before Christmas. Once again the Passion narrative brings us to Holy Week, where the special readings are largely traditional.

POST-EASTER

The Old Testament readings from 1 Kings about the kingdom established by David may be thought appropriate during the season when the Church rejoices at the victory of David's greater Son. The Epistles suitably come from Ephesians and then Revelation, while the Gospels concentrate on St John, which continues into the Pentecost period.

PENTECOST

In the Old Testament, Ezekiel and Daniel are followed by Ezra, Nehemiah, Jonah, Haggai, Zechariah, and then Proverbs. The Epistles read through Philippians, the Pastorals, Philemon, Hebrews, and 1 Peter, and then conclude with Acts, while the Gospels continue the reading of St John with the systematic reading of St Matthew. Again at the end of Pentecost there are selected readings from the Apocrypha given as alternatives to Old Testament passages, mainly from the Wisdom literature; while the Gospel readings include excerpts from the Sermon on the Mount (St Matthew) and the Sermon on the Plain (St Luke).

Apart from a short selection in the 20th week after Pentecost in Year 1, Chronicles has been omitted, since corresponding passages will have been read from Samuel and Kings.

THE LECTIONARY

	O.T.	EPISTLES	GOSPELS
F	24.52–67	12.13–17	8.12–30
S	25.19–34	13. 1–10	8.31–47

5th before Christmas

	Gen.	Rev.	John
M	27. 1–29	13.11–18	8.48–59
T	27.30–46	14. 1–13	9. 1–12
W	28.10–22	14.14–20	9.13–29
T	29. 1–30	15	9.30–41
F	32. 1–23	16. 1–11	10. 1–21
S	32.24—33.11	16.12–21	10.22–42

4th before Christmas
(Advent 1)

	Isa.	Rev.	Matt.
M	1. 1– 9	17. 1– 6	23. 1–12
T	1.10–20	17. 7–18	23.13–22
W	1.21–31	19. 1–10	23.23–28
T	2. 1–11	19.11–16 (or 21)	23.29–39
F	2.12–22	20. 1–10	24. 1–14
S	3. 1– 8	20.11–15	24.15–28

3rd before Christmas
(Advent 2)

	Isa.	Rev.	Matt.
M	3.13—4. 1	21. 1– 8	24.29–34
T	4. 2– 6	21. 9–14	24.35–42
W	5. 1– 7	21.15–21	24.43–51
T	5. 8–23	21.22—22. 5	25. 1–13
F	5.24–30	22. 6–13	25.14–30
S	6. 1–12	22.14–21	25.31–46

2nd before Christmas
(Advent 3)

	1 Kings	Col.	
M	17. 1–16	1. 1–14	Luke 1. 5–25
T	18. 1–16	1.15–29	3. 1–14
W	18.17–29	2. 1–15	3.15–22
T	18.30–46	2.16—3.11	Matt. 11. 2– 6

41

	O.T.	EPISTLES	GOSPELS
F	19. 1– 8	3.12–25	11. 7–19
S	19. 9–21	4	John 5.30– 6

(These are John Baptist passages. Readings for 18–31 December will take priority)

1st before Christmas (Advent 4) *to Christmas 1 (18–31 December)*

Dec.

18	Isa.	7.10–17	Philemon	Luke	1.26–38
19		28.14–22	2 John		1.39–45
20		29.13–24	3 John		1.46–56
21		30.15–21	Phil. 1. 1– 8		1.57–66
22		32. 1– 8	1. 9–18		1.67–80
23		35	1.19–26	Matt. 3. 1–10	
24		52. 1–10	1.27—2.4		1.18–25

Christmas Day

		65.17–25	2. 5–11	Luke	2.15–20
26		40. 1–11	2.12–18		2.21–25
27		40.12–24	2.19–30		2.25–35
28		40.25–31	3. 1–11		2.36–40
29		41. 1–13	3.12—4.1	Matt. 2. 1–12	
30		41.14–20	4. 2– 9		2.13–23
31	Deut.	11.11–21	4.10–20	Luke 2.41–52	

(If any of the days from 18–24 December falls on a Sunday, Luke 1.46–56 may be omitted if it is used as a canticle, or Matt. 3.1–10)

Christmas 1

M	Isa.	42. 1– 9	Eph. 1. 1–14	Matt.	3. 1–17
T		42.10–25	1.15–23		4. 1–11
W		43. 1– 7	2. 1–10		4.12–25
T		43. 8–21	2.11–22		5. 1–12

42

	O.T.	EPISTLES	GOSPELS
F	43.22–28	3. 1–13	5.13–20
S	44. 1– 5	3.14–21	5.21–26

(Christmas 1 etc. will fit in after 31 December and will not take precedence)

Christmas 2

	O.T.	EPISTLES	GOSPELS
M	Isa. 44. 6–22	Eph. 4. 1–16	Matt. 5.27–37
T	44.23–28	4.17–32	5.38–48
W	45. 1– 8	5. 1–14	6. 1–15
T	45. 9–13	5.15–33	6.16–34
F	45.14–17	6. 1– 9	7. 1–12
S	45.18–25	6.10–24	7.13–29

Christmas 3

	O.T.	EPISTLES	GOSPELS
M	Isa. 46	1 Tim. 1. 1–17	Matt. 8. 1–13
T	47. 1– 9	1.18—2.16	8.14–22
W	47.10–15	3. 1–16	8.23–34
T	48. 1–11	4. 1–16	9. 1– 8
F	48.12–22	5. 1–16	9. 9–17
S	49. 1– 6	5.17–25	9.18–26

Christmas 4

	O.T.	EPISTLES	GOSPELS
M	Isa. 49. 7–13	1 Tim. 6. 1–10	Matt. 9.27–38
T	49.14–21	6.11–21	10. 1– 8
W	49.22–26	2 Tim. 1. 1–14	10. 9–15
T	50. 1–11	1.15—2.13	10.16–23
F	51. 1–11	2.14–26	10.24–33
S	51.12–33	3. 1–17	10.34—11.1

Christmas 5

	O.T.	EPISTLES	GOSPELS
M	Isa. 52.13—53. 6	2 Tim. 4. 1–18	Matt. 11. 2– 6
T	53. 7–12	Titus 1	11. 7–19
W	54. 1–10	2	11.20–30
T	54.11–17	3	12. 1– 8
F	56. 1– 8	1 John 1—2.6	12. 9–21
S	57.15–19	2. 7–17	12.22–37

	O.T.	EPISTLES	GOSPELS

Christmas 6

M	Isa. 58. 1– 5	1 John 2.18–29	Matt. 12.38–50
T	58. 6–12	3. 1–10	13. 1– 9
W	58.13–14	3.11–24	13.10–23
T	59. 1– 8	4	13.24–33
F	59. 9–15a	5. 1–12	13.34–43
S	59.15b–21	5.13–21	13.44–58

9th before Easter

M	Jer. 1. 1–10	Gal. 1. 1–10	Matt. 14. 1–12
T	1.11–19	1.11–24	14.13–21
W	2. 4–13	2. 1–10	14.22–36
T	3. 6–18	2.11–21	15. 1–20
F	4. 5–14	3. 1–14	15.21–28
S	4.19–31	3.15–22	15.29–39

8th before Easter

M	Jer. 5. 1– 9	Gal. 3.23–29	Matt. 16. 1–12
T	5.20–31	4. 1–11	16.13–20
W	6. 9–15	4.12–20	16.21–28
T	6.22–30	4.21—5.1	17. 1–13
F	7. 1–15	5. 2–12	17.14–27
S	7.21–28	5.13–25	18. 1–20

7th before Easter

M	Jer. 8.18—9.3	Gal. 6. 1–10	Matt. 18.21–35
T	9.17–24	6.11–18	19. 1–15

Ash Wednesday

	14. 7– 9	2 Cor. 7. 2–10	Mark 2.13–22
T	10. 1–10	Jas. 1. 1–11	Matt. 19.16–30
F	10.11–16	1.12–27	20. 1–16
S	10.17–24	2. 1–13	20.17–28

6th before Easter (Lent 1)

M	Jer. 12. 1– 6	Jas. 2.14–26	Matt. 20.29–34

	O.T.	EPISTLES	GOSPELS
T	13.20–27	3. 1–12	21. 1–11
W	15.10–21	3.13–18	21.12–17
T	17. 9–18	4. 1–12	21.18–32
F	18. 1–12	4.13—5.6	21.33–46
S	18.13–23	5. 7–20	22. 1–14

5th before
Easter
(Lent 2)

	O.T.	EPISTLES	GOSPELS
M	Jer. 19. 1–13	Heb. 1	Matt. 22.15–22
T	19.14—20–6	2. 1– 9	22.23–33
W	20. 7–18	2.10–18	22.34–46
T	21. 1–10	3. 1– 6	23. 1–12
F	22.13–19	3. 7–19	23.13–24
S	22.20–30	4. 1–10	23.25–39

4th before
Easter
(Lent 3)

	O.T.	EPISTLES	GOSPELS
M	Jer. 23. 1– 8	Heb. 4.11–16	Matt. 24. 1–14
T	23.16–29	5. 1–10	24.15–28
W	24	5.11—6.8	24.29–34
T	25. 1–14	6. 9–20	24.35–51
F	26. 1– 9	7. 1–10	25. 1–13
S	26.10–24	7.11–28	25.14–30

3rd before
Easter
(Lent 4)

	O.T.	EPISTLES	GOSPELS
M	Jer. 29. 1,4–14	Heb. 8	Matt. 25.31–46
T	30.10–22	9. 1–14	26. 1–13
W	31. 1–14	9.15–28	26.14–29
T	31.15–22	10. 1–18	26.30–35
F	31.23–34	10.19–39	26.36–46
S	31.35–40	11. 1–12	26.47–56

2nd before
Easter
(Passion Sunday)

	O.T.	EPISTLES	GOSPELS
M	Jer. 32. 1–15	Heb. 11.13–22	Matt. 26.57–68

	O.T.	EPISTLES	GOSPELS
T	36. 1– 8,27–32	11.23–31	26.69–75
W	37.11–21	11.32–40	27. 1–10
T	38. 1–13	12. 1–11	27.11–26
F	39. 1–18	12.12–29	27.27–44
S	42. 1–12	13. 1–21	27.45–66

1st before
Easter
(Palm Sunday)
Holy Week

		O.T.	EPISTLES		GOSPELS	
M	Lam.	1. 1–11	Gal.	6.11–18	John 14. 1–11
T		2.11–17	Rom.	5. 6–11	14.12–31
W		3.40–51		5.12–19	15. 1–17
T	Exod.	24. 1–11	Eph.	2.11–18	15.18–27

Good Friday

		O.T.	EPISTLES		GOSPELS
	Lam.	5.15–22	Col.	1.18–23	Mark 15.21–41
S	Gen.	7.11–18	1 John	5. 4–10	15.42–47

Easter Week

		O.T.	EPISTLES		GOSPELS
M	Isa.	26. 1– 9	1 Pet.	1. 1–12	Mark 16. 9–18
T		26.13–19		1.13–25	Luke 24. 1–12
W	2 Kings	4.18–37		2. 1–10	24.13–35
T	Ezek.	37. 1–14		2.11–25	24.36–49
F	Zech.	8. 1– 8		3. 1–12	Matt. 28. 1–10
S	Zeph.	3.14–20		3.13–22	28.11–20

Easter 1

		O.T.	EPISTLES		GOSPELS
M	Exod.	1. 1–22	1 Pet.	4. 1–11	Mark 1. 1–13
T		2. 1–25		4.12–19	1.14–20
W		3. 1–12		5	1.21–28
T		3.13–22	2 Pet.	1. 1–11	1.29–39
F		4. 1–17		1.12–21	1.40–45
S		4.18–31		3. 8–13	2. 1–12

Easter 2

		O.T.	EPISTLES		GOSPELS
M	Exod.	5. 1–14	1 Thess.	1	Mark 2.13–17
T		5.15–23		2. 1–12	2.18–22
W		6. 1–13		2.13–20	2.23–28
T		6.28—7.13		3	3. 1– 6
F		7.14–24		4. 1–12	3. 7–19a

	O.T.	EPISTLES	GOSPELS
S	7.25—8.15	4.13–18	3.19b–30

Easter 3

	O.T.	EPISTLES	GOSPELS
M	Exod. 8.16–32	1 Thess. 5. 1–11	Mark 3.31–35
T	9. 1–12	5.12–28	4. 1–20
W	9.13–35	2 Thess. 1	4.21–34
T	10. 1–11	2. 1–12	4.35–41
F	10.12–29	2.13–17	5. 1–20
S	11. 1–10	3	5.21–34

Easter 4

	O.T.	EPISTLES	GOSPELS
M	Exod. 12. 1–13	Rom. 1. 1–17	Mark 5.35–43
T	12.14–27	1.18–32	6. 1– 6
W	12.28–36	2. 1–16	6. 7–13
T	12.37–51	2.17–29	6.14–29
F	13. 1–16	3. 1–20	6.30–44
S	13.17—14.4	3.21–31	6.45–56

Easter 5

	O.T.	EPISTLES	GOSPELS
M	Exod. 14. 5–20	Rom. 4. 1–12	Mark 7. 1–13
T	14.21–31	4.13–25	7.14–23
W	15.22–27	5. 1–11	7.24–30

Ascension Day

	O.T.	EPISTLES	GOSPELS
	2 Kings 2. 1–15	Heb. 9.11–15	16.14–20
F	Exod. 16. 1–21	Rom. 5.12–21	7.31–37
S	16.22–36	6. 1–14	8. 1–10

Easter 6

	O.T.	EPISTLES	GOSPELS
M	Exod. 17	Rom. 6. 15–23	Mark 8.11–21
T	18. 1–12	7. 1–12	8.22–26
W	18.13–27	7.13–25	8.27–33
T	19. 1–15	8. 1–17	8.34—9.1
F	19.16–25	8.18–30	9. 2–13
S	20. 1–17	8.31–39	9.14–29

Pentecost

	O.T.	EPISTLES	GOSPELS
M	Num. 11.16–30	Rom. 9. 1–13	John 14. 1–11
T	1 Sam. 10. 1–10	9.14–29	14.12–31
W	Ezek. 11.14–20	9.30—10.10	15. 1–17

47

	O.T.	EPISTLES	GOSPELS
T	Mic. 3. 1– 8	10.11–21	15.18–27
F	Isa. 61. 1– 7	11. 1–24	16. 1–15
S	Jer. 31.31–34	11.25–36	16.16–33

Pentecost 1

	O.T.	EPISTLES	GOSPELS
M	Exod. 20.18–26	Rom. 12. 1– 8	Mark 9.30–37
T	24. 1– 8	12. 9–21	9.38–50
W	24. 9–18	13. 1–14	10. 1–12
T	32. 1–14	14. 1–12	10.13–22
F	32.15–29	14.13–23	10.23–31
S	34. 1–10	15. 1–13	10.32–45

Pentecost 2

	O.T.	EPISTLES	GOSPELS
M	Num. 9.15–23	Rom. 15.14–22	Mark 10.46–52
T	12	15.23–33	11. 1–11
W	13.17–33	Acts 1. 1–14	11.12–19
T	14. 1–10a	1.15–26	11.20–26
F	14.10b–25	2. 1–13	11.27–33
S	20. 1–13	2.14–36	12. 1–12

Pentecost 3

	O.T.	EPISTLES	GOSPELS
M	Num. 21. 4– 9	Acts 2.37–47	Mark 12.13–17
T	22. 2–15,21–35	3. 1–10	12.18–27
W	22.36—23.12	3.11—4.4	12.28–34
T	23.13–30	4. 5–22	12.35–44
F	24. 1– 9	4.23–31	13. 1–13
S	24.10–25	4.32—5.11	13.14–27

Pentecost 4

	O.T.	EPISTLES	GOSPELS
M	Deut. 1. 1– 8	Acts 5.12–26	Mark 13.28–37
T	4. 1–13	5.27–42	14. 1– 9
W	4.14–24	6. 1–15	14.10–25
T	4.25–35	7. 1–16	14.26–42
F	5. 1–21	7.17–36	14.43–52
S	5.22–33	7.37–53	14.53–65

Pentecost 5

	O.T.	EPISTLES	GOSPELS
M	Deut. 6. 1–12	Acts 7.54—8.3	Mark 14.66–72
T	6.13–25	8. 4–25	15. 1–15

	O.T.	EPISTLES	GOSPELS
W	7. 6–11	8.26–40	15.16–32
T	8. 1–10	9. 1–19a	15.33–47
F	8.11–20	9.19b–31	16. 1– 8
S	9. 1– 5	9.32–43	16. 9–20

Pentecost 6

	O.T.	EPISTLES	GOSPELS
M	Deut. 10.11–22	Acts 10. 1–16	Luke 1. 1–25
T	11. 1–12	10.17–33	1.26–38
W	12. 1–11	10.34–48	1.39–56
T	13. 1– 5	11. 1–18	1.57–66
F	15. 1–11	11.19–30	1.67–80
S	18.15–22	12. 1–11	2. 1– 7

Pentecost 7

	O.T.	EPISTLES	GOSPELS
M	Deut. 26. 1–11	Acts 12.12–25	Luke 2. 8–20
T	28. 1–14	13. 1–12	2.21–32
W	30. 1–10	13.13–41	2.33–40
T	30.11–20	13.42—14.7	2.41–52
F	32. 1–12	14. 8–28	3. 1–14
S	34	15. 1–21	3.15–22

Pentecost 8

	O.T.	EPISTLES	GOSPELS
M	Josh. 1. 1–11	Acts 15.22–35	Luke 4. 1–13
T	2	15.36—16.5	4.14–30
W	3. 7–17	16. 6–24	4.31–44
T	4. 1–11	16.25–40	5. 1–11
F	5.13—6.11	17. 1–15	5.12–26
S	6.12–23	17.16–34	5.27–39

Pentecost 9

	O.T.	EPISTLES	GOSPELS
M	Josh. 7. 1–15	Acts 18. 1–21	Luke 6. 1–11
T	7.16–26	18.22—19.7	6.12–26
W	8.10–23	19. 8–20	6.27–38
T	9. 3–21	19.21–41	6.39–49
F	24. 1–13	20. 1–16	7. 1–10
S	24.14–25	20.17–38	7.11–23

Pentecost 10

	O.T.	EPISTLES	GOSPELS
M	Judges 2.11–23	Acts 21. 1–16	Luke 7.24–35

	O.T.	EPISTLES	GOSPELS
T		4. 1–21	21.17–26	7.36–50
W		5. 1–18	21.27–39	8. 1–15
T		5.19–31	21.40—22.21	8.16–25
F		6. 1,11–32	22.22—23.11	8.26–39
S		7. 1–23	23.12–25	8.40–56

Pentecost 11

M	Judges	9. 1–21	Acts	24. 1–23	Luke	9. 1– 9
T		9.44–51		24.24—25.12		9.10–17
W		11. 1– 6,29–40		25.13–27		9.18–27
T		13		26. 1–23		9.28–36
F		14. 1–14		26.24–32		9.37–43
S		14.15–20		27. 1– 8		9.44–50

Pentecost 12

M	Judges	15. 1– 8	Acts	27. 9–26	Luke	9.51–62
T		15. 9–20		27.27–44		10. 1–16
W		16. 1–22		28. 1–15		10.17–24
T		16.23–31		28.16–31		10.25–37
F		17	1 Cor.	1. 1– 9		10.38–42
S		18. 1–20,27–31		1.10–25		11. 1–13

Pentecost 13

M	Ruth	1. 1–14	1 Cor.	1.26—2.5	Luke	11.14–20
T		1.15–22		2. 6–16		11.21–28
W		2. 1–13		3. 1– 9		11.29–36
T		2.14–23		3.10–23		11.37–44
F		3		4. 1–13		11.45–54
S		4. 1–17		4.14–21		12. 1–12

Pentecost 14

M	Joel	1. 1–13	1 Cor.	5	Luke	12.13–21
T		1.14–20		6. 1–11		12.22–31
W		2. 1–11		6.12–20		12.32–40
T		2.12–22		7. 1–24		12.41–48
F		2.23–32		7.25–40		12.49–59
S		3. 9–21		8		13. 1– 9

Pentecost 15

| M | Nahum | 1. 1–10 | 1 Cor. | 9. 1–14 | Luke | 13.10–21 |

		O.T.	EPISTLES	GOSPELS
T		2. 1,3–12	9.15–27	13.22–35
W		3. 1–3,12–19	10. 1–13	14. 1–11
T	Hab.	1. 5–14	10.14—11.1	14.12–24
F		2. 1–19	11. 2–22	14.25–35
S		3. 1–19	11.23–34	15. 1–10

Pentecost 16

		O.T.	EPISTLES	GOSPELS
M	Job	1. 1–12	1 Cor. 12. 1–11	Luke 15.11–32
T		1.13–22	12.12–31	16. 1–18
W		2	13	16.19–31
T		3. 1–17	14. 1–12	17. 1–10
F		4. 1–17	14.13–25	17.11–19
S		6. 1–13	14.26–40	17.20–37

Pentecost 17

		O.T.	EPISTLES	GOSPELS
M	Job	13. 1–15	1 Cor. 15. 1–11	Luke 18. 1–14
T		14. 1–14	15.12–19	18.15–30
W		19.14–27	15.20–34	18.31–43
T		28. 1–11	15.35–49	19. 1–10
F		28.12–28	15.50–58	19.11–27
S		31.13–37	2 Cor. 1. 1–14	19.28–40

Pentecost 18

		O.T.	EPISTLES	GOSPELS
M	Job	38. 1–21	2 Cor. 1.15—2.4	Luke 19.41–48
T		38.22–41	2. 5–17	20. 1– 8
W		39	3	20. 9–26
T		40	4	20.27–40
F		41	5	20.41—21.4
S		42	6. 1–11	22. 1–13

Pentecost 19

		O.T.	EPISTLES	GOSPELS
M	Eccles.	1	2 Cor. 6.12–18	Luke 22.14–23
T		3. 1–15	7	22.24–34
W		5. 1–12	8. 1–15	22.35–46
T		7. 1–14	8.16—9.5	22.47–62
F		9. 1–16	9. 6–15	22.63–71
S		11. 9—12.13	10	23. 1–12

	O.T.		EPISTLES	GOSPELS

Pentecost 20

	Wisd.	or 1 Chron.	2 Cor.	Luke
M	1	28. 1–10	11. 1–15	23.13–25
T	2. 1–20	28.11–21	11.16–33	23.26–43
W	2.21—3.9	29. 1–9	12	23.44–56a
T	4. 7–17	29.10–19	13	23.56b—24.12
F	6. 1–21	29.20–30	Jude 1–16	24.13–35
		2 Chron.		
S	7.15—8.1	1. 1– 6	17–25	24.36–53

Pentecost 21

	Wisd.	or Song of Sol.	Eph.	Matt.
M	9	1. 9—2.7	1. 1–14	5. 1–16
T	10.15—11.10	2. 8–17	1.15–23	5.17–30
W	11.21—12.2	3	2. 1–10	5.33–48
T	12.12–21	5. 2—6.3	2.11–22	7. 1–11
	Baruch			
F	3. 1–14	7.10—8,4	3. 1–13	7.12–20
S	4.36—5.9	8. 5– 7	3.14–21	7.21–29

SECOND YEAR

	O.T.	EPISTLES	GOSPELS

9th before Christmas

	O.T.	EPISTLES	GOSPELS
M	Gen. 37. 1–11	Rom. 1. 1–17	Mark 1. 1–13
T	37.12–24	1.18–32	1.14–20
W	37.25–36	2. 1–16	1.21–28
T	39. 1– 6a	2.17–29	1.29–39
F	39. 6b–23	3. 1–20	1.40–45
S	40	3.21–31	2. 1–12

8th before Christmas

M	Gen. 41. 1–13	Rom. 4. 1–12	Mark 2.13–17
T	41.14–45	4.13–25	2.18–22
W	41.46–57	5. 1–11	2.23–28
T	42.11–17	5.12–21	3. 1– 6
F	42.18–28	6. 1–14	3. 7–19a
S	42.29–38	6.15–23	3.19b–30

7th before Christmas

M	Gen. 43. 1–15	Rom. 7. 1–12	Mark 3.31–35
T	43.16–34	7.13–25	4. 1–20
W	44. 1–17	8. 1–11	4,21–34
T	44.18–34	8.12–17	4.35–41
F	45. 1–15	8.18–30	5. 1–20
S	45.16–28	8.31–39	5.21–34

6th before Christmas

M	Gen. 46. 1– 7,28–33	Rom. 9. 1–13	Mark 5.35–43
T	47. 1–26	9.14–29	6. 1– 6
W	47.27—48.9	9.30—10.4	6. 7–13
T	48.10–22	10. 5–13	6.14–29
F	49.29—50.14	10.14–21	6.30–44
S	50.15–26	11. 1–12	6.45–56

	O.T.	EPISTLES	GOSPELS

5th before
Christmas

M	Isa.	9. 8–17	Rom. 11.13–24	Mark	7. 1–13
T		9.18—10.4	11.25–36		7.14–23
W		10. 5–19	12. 1– 8		7.24–30
T		10.20–27	12. 9–21		7.31–37
F		11.10–16	13. 1– 7		8. 1–10
S		12	13. 8–14		8.11–21

4th before
Christmas
(Advent 1)

M	Isa.	13. 1–13	Rom. 14. 1–12	Luke	17.20–37
T		14. 3–15	14.13–23		19.11–27
W		15. 1—16.5	15. 1– 6		19.28–40
T		19. 1–25	15. 7–13		19.41–48
F		24. 1–23	15.14–22		20. 9–18
S		26. 1–19	15.23–33		20.19–26

3rd before
Christmas
(Advent 2)

M	Dan.	7. 1–14	1 Thess. 1	Luke	20.27–40
T		7.15–27	2. 1–12		20.41—21.4
W	Zeph.	3.11–20	2.13–20		21. 5– 9
T	Zech.	9. 9–12	3		21.10–19
F		13	4. 1–12		21.20–28
S		14. 1– 9	4.13–18		21.29–36

2nd before
Christmas
(Advent 3)

M	Mal.	2.17—3.6	1 Thess. 5. 1–11	Matt.	3. 1–12
T		4	5.12–28	Luke	7.18–23
W	1 Kings	21. 1–16	2 Thess. 1		7.24–28
T		21.17–29	2. 1–12		7.29–35
F	Isa.	40. 3– 8	2.13–17	Matt.	7.13–21

	O.T.	EPISTLES	GOSPELS
S	40. 9–11	3	7.22–27

These are John Baptist passages. Readings for 18–31 December will take priority.

1st before Christmas (Advent 4) *to Christmas 1 (18–31 December)*

Dec.

	O.T.	EPISTLES	GOSPELS
18	Isa. 55. 1– 5	Phil. 2. 5–11	John 1.15–28
19	55. 6–13	4. 4– 9	1.29–37
20	56. 1– 5	Titus 2.11–15	3.22–30
21	57.14–21	3. 4– 7	3.31–36
22	58. 6–12	Rom. 1. 1– 6	5.39–47
23	59. 1–15a	Gal. 4. 1– 7	7.37–44
24	59.15b–21	Eph. 3.14–21	13. 1–17

Christmas Day

	O.T.	EPISTLES	GOSPELS
	65.17–25	1 John 1	3.16–21
26	42. 1– 9	2. 1–11	16.31—17.5
27	49. 1– 6	2.12–17	19.25–27
28	50. 4–11	3. 1–10	15.11–25
29	52.13—53.6	4.17–21	12. 1–12
30	53. 7–12	5. 1–12	12.20–33
31	51. 1–11	5.13–21	12.34–50

Christmas 1

	O.T.	EPISTLES	GOSPELS
M	Isa. 60. 1–14	1 Cor. 1. 1– 9	Luke 3. 1–14
T	60.15–22	1.10–25	3.15–22
W	61. 1– 7	1.26—2.5	4. 1–13
T	61. 8–11	2. 6–16	4.14–30
F	62. 1– 5	3. 1– 9	4.41–44
S	62. 6–12	3.10–23	5. 1–11

Christmas 1 etc., will fit in after 31 December and will not take precedence.

55

O.T.	EPISTLES	GOSPELS

Christmas 2

M	Isa. 63. 1– 6	1 Cor. 4. 1–13	Luke	5.12–36
T	63. 7–14	4.14–21		5.27–39
W	63.15—64.5a	5		6. 1–11
T	64. 5b–12	6. 1–11		6.12–26
F	65. 1–16	6.12–20		6.27–38
S	66. 1– 2	7. 1–24		6.39–49

Christmas 3

M	Amos 1. 1– 5	1 Cor. 7.25–40	Luke	7. 1–10
T	2. 1– 5	8		7.11–23
W	2. 6–16	9. 1–14		7.24–35
T	3. 1– 8	9.15–27		7.36–50
F	4. 4–13	10. 1–13		8. 1–15
S	5. 1–15	10.14—11.1		8.16–25

Christmas 4

M	Amos 5.16–24	1 Cor. 11.2–22	Luke	8.26–39
T	6. 1– 8	11.23–34		8.40–56
W	7. 1– 9	12. 1–11		9. 1– 9
T	7.10–17	12.12–31		9.10–17
F	8. 1–12	13		9.18–27
S	9. 8–15	14. 1–12		9.28–43

Christmas 5

M	Hos. 1. 1—2.1	1 Cor. 14.13–25		9.43–50
T	2. 2–15	14.26–40		9.51–62
W	2.18—3.5	15. 1–19		10. 1–16
T	6. 1– 6	15.20–34		10.17–24
F	11. 1– 9	15.35–49		10.25–42
S	14	15.50–58		11. 1–13

Christmas 6

M	Mic. 1. 1– 9	2 Pet. 1. 1–11	Luke	11.14–28
T	2. 1– 4,12–13	1.12–21		11.29–44
W	3	2. 1–10a		11.45–54
T	4. 1– 5	2.10b–22		12. 1–12

	O.T.	EPISTLES	GOSPELS
F	4. 8—5.2	3. 1–10	12.13–34
S	6. 1– 8	3.11–18	12.35–48

9th before Easter

	O.T.	EPISTLES	GOSPELS
M 1 Sam.	1. 1–20	2 Cor. 1. 1–14	Luke 12.49–59
T	1.21—2.11	1.15—2.4	13. 1–17
W	3. 1–19	2. 5–17	13.18–35
T	4. 1–18	3	14. 1–11
F	5	4	14.12–24
S	6. 1–16	5	14.25–35

8th before Easter

	O.T.	EPISTLES	GOSPELS
M 1 Sam.	9. 1–14	2 Cor. 6. 1–11	Luke 15. 1–10
T	9.15—10.1	6.12–18	15.11–32
W	14. 1–15	7	16. 1–18
T	14.24–46	8. 1–15	16.19–31
F	15. 1–11	8.16—9.5	17. 1–19
S	15.12–23	9. 6–15	17.20–37

7th before Easter

	O.T.	EPISTLES	GOSPELS
M 1 Sam.	16. 1–13	2 Cor. 10	Luke 18. 1–14
T	16.14–23	11. 1–15	18.15–30

Ash Wednesday

	O.T.	EPISTLES	GOSPELS
	Joel 2.12–17	1 Cor. 9.19–27	Matt. 6.16–21
T 1 Sam.	17. 1–25	2 Cor. 11.16–33	Luke 18.31–43
F	17.26–50	12	22. 1–23
S	18. 1–16	13	22.24–38

6th before Easter (Lent 1)

	O.T.	EPISTLES	GOSPELS
M 1 Sam.	19. 1–18	Gal. 1. 1–10	Luke 22.39–53
T	20. 1–23	1.11–24	22.54–71

	O.T.	EPISTLES	GOSPELS
W	20.24–42	2. 1–10	23. 1–12
T	24	2.11–21	23.13–31
F	31	3. 1–14	23.32–43
S 2 Sam.	1. 1–27	3.15–22	23.44–56a

5th before
Easter
(Lent 2)

M 2 Sam.	2. 1–11	Gal. 3.23–29	Mark 9. 2–13
T	5. 1–10,17–25	4. 1–11	9.14–29
W	6. 1–19	4.12–20	9.30–50
T	7. 1–13	4.21—5.1	10. 1–12
F	7.18–29	5. 2–12	10.13–22
S	9	5.13–25	10.23–31

4th before
Easter
(Lent 3)

M 2 Sam.	11. 1–17	Gal. 6. 1–10	Mark 10.32–45
T	11.18–27	6.11–18	10.46–52
W	12. 1–14	Col. 1. 1–14	11. 1–11
T	12.15–25	1.15–29	11.12–19
F	15. 1–15	2. 1–15	11.20–26
S	15.16–37	2.16—3.11	11.27–33

3rd before
Easter
(Lent 4)

M 2 Sam.	16. 1–14	Col. 3.12–25	Mark 12. 1–12
T	17. 1–14	4	12.13–27
W	17.15–23	Jas. 1. 1–11	12.28–44
T	18. 1–18	1.12–18	13. 1–13
F	18.19–33	1.19–27	13.14–27
S	19. 1–15	2. 1–13	13.28–37

2nd before
Easter
(Passion Sunday)

M 2 Sam.	19.16–30	Jas. 2.14–26	Mark 14. 1–11
T	19.31–43	3. 1–12	14.12–31

	O.T.	EPISTLES	GOSPELS
W	23. 1– 7	3.13–18	14.32–52
T	23. 8–23	4. 1–12	14.53–65
F	24. 1–14	4.13—5.6	14.66–72
S	24.15–25	5. 7–20	15. 1–20

1st before
Easter
(Palm Sunday)

		O.T.	EPISTLES		GOSPELS	
M	Isa.	5. 1– 7	Heb.	2. 9–18	John	16. 1–15
T	Wisd.	1. 1,12–16		8. 1– 6		16.16–33
	or Jer.	11.18–20				
W	Isa.	63. 1– 9		9.11–15		17. 1–19
T	Exod.	13. 3–10		9.16–28		17.19–26

Good Friday

	Gen.	22. 1–18		10. 1–10	Matt.	27.27–56
					or John	18
						and
						19. 1–37
S	Job	19.21–27	1 Pet.	4. 1– 6		19.38–42

Easter Week

M	Exod.	15. 1–12	Eph.	1. 1–14	John	20. 1–10
T		15.13–21		1.15–23		20.11–23
W	Isa.	25. 1– 9		2. 1–10		20.24–31
T	Jer.	31. 1–14		2.11–22		21. 1–14
F	Job	14. 1–14		3. 1–13		21.15–19
S	Mic.	7. 7–20		3.14–21		21.20–25

Easter 1

M	1 Kings	1. 5–31	Eph.	4. 1–16	John	1. 1–18
T		1.38–53		4.17–32		1.19–34
W		2. 1–12		5. 1–14		1.35–51
T		3. 3–15		5.15–33		2. 1–12
F		5. 1–12		6. 1– 9		2.13–25
S		6. 1–14		6.10–24		3. 1–15

Easter 2

M	1 Kings	8. 1–21	Rev.	1. 1– 8	John	3.16–22
T		11. 1–13		1. 9–20		3.22–36

	O.T.	EPISTLES	GOSPELS
W	11.26–40	2. 1–11	4. 1–26
T	11.43—12.16	2.12–17	4.27–42
F	12.25–33	2.18–29	4.43–54
S	13. 1–10	3. 1– 6	5. 1–18

Easter 3

	O.T.	EPISTLES	GOSPELS
M 1 Kings	20. 1–21	Rev. 3. 7–13	John 5.19–29
T	20.22–43	3.14–22	5.30–40
W	21, 1–16	4	5.41–47
T	21.17–29	5	6. 1–15
F	22. 1–28	6	6.16–29
S	22.29–40	7. 1– 8	6.30–40

Easter 4

	O.T.	EPISTLES	GOSPELS
M 2 Kings	2. 1–15	Rev. 7. 9–17	John 6.41–51
T	3. 4–24	11. 1–13	6.52–59
W	4. 1–17	11.14–19	6.60–71
T	5. 1–19a	12. 1– 6	7. 1–13
F	5.19b–27	12. 7–17	7.14–24
S	6. 8–23	13. 1–10	7.25–36

Easter 5

	O.T.	EPISTLES	GOSPELS
M 2 Kings	6.24—7.2	Rev. 13.11–18	John 7.37–52
T	7. 3–20	14. 1–13	8.12–20
W	9. 1–13	14.14–20	8.21–30

Ascension Day

		O.T.	EPISTLES	GOSPELS
Song of 3 Chil.		29–37	Heb. 9.19–28	Mark 16.14–20
or Ezek.		1. 4– 5,26–8		
F 2 Kings		9.14–37	Rev. 19, 1–10	John 8.31–47
S		10.18–28	19.11–16 (*or* 21)	8.48–59

Easter 6

	O.T.	EPISTLES	GOSPELS
M 2 Kings	17. 1–14	Rev. 20. 1–15	John 9. 1–12
T	18. 1–12	21. 1– 8	9.13–23
W	18.13–25	21. 9–21	9.24–41
T	19. 1–19	21.22—22.5	10. 1–16
F	19.20–37	22, 6–13	10.17–30
S	20. 1–20	22.14–21	10.31–42

	O.T.	EPISTLES	GOSPELS

Pentecost

	O.T.	EPISTLES	GOSPELS
M	Num. 27.12–23	Phil. 1. 1– 8	Luke 1.26–38
T	2 Sam. 23. 1– 5	1. 9–18	2.22–32
W	Ezek. 36.22–28	1.19–26	3.15–22
T	Zech. 4. 1–10	1.27—2.4	4.16–21
F	Isa. 44. 1– 8	2. 5–18	11. 5–13
S	Ezek. 37. 1–14	2.19–30	12. 8–12

Pentecost 1

	O.T.	EPISTLES	GOSPELS
M	2 Kings 22. 3–20	Phil. 3. 1–11	John 11. 1–16
T	23. 1–10	3.12—4.1	11.17–37
W	23.21–30	4. 2– 9	11.38–45
T	24. 8–17	4.10–20	11.46–57
F	24.18—25.12	1 Tim. 1. 1–17	12. 1–11
S	25.22–30	1.18—2.15	12.12–19

Pentecost 2

	O.T.	EPISTLES	GOSPELS
M	Ezek. 1. 1–14	1 Tim. 3	John 12.20–36
T	1.15—2.2	4	12.37–50
W	2. 3—3.11	5. 1–16	13. 1–11
T	3.12–27	5.17–25	13.12–20
F	5. 5–12	6. 1–10	13.21–30
S	8. 1–12	6.11–21	13.31–38

Pentecost 3

	O.T.	EPISTLES	GOSPELS
M	Ezek. 9	2 Tim. 1. 1–14	John 14. 1–11
T	10. 1–19	1.15—2.13	14.12–31
W	11.14–25	2.14–26	15. 1–17
T	14.12–23	3	15.18–27
F	18	4. 1–18	16. 1–15
S	24.15–27	Titus 1	16.16–33

Pentecost 4

	O.T.	EPISTLES	GOSPELS
M	Ezek. 26. 1–14	Titus 2	John 17. 1–11
T	28. 1–10	3	17.12–18
W	32.17–32	Philemon	17.19–26
T	33. 1– 9	Heb. 1	18. 1–11

	O.T.	EPISTLES	GOSPELS
F	33.10–20	2. 1– 9	18.12–18, 25–27
S	33.21–33	2.10–18	18.19–24

Pentecost 5

	O.T.	EPISTLES	GOSPELS
M	Ezek. 34. 1–10	Heb. 3	John 18.28–40
T	34.11–16	4. 1–10	19. 1–16a
W	34.17–31	4.11–16	19.16b–24
T	36. 1–15	5	19.25–30
F	36.16–32	6. 1–12	19.31–37
S	36.33–38	6.13–20	19.38–42

Pentecost 6

	O.T.	EPISTLES	GOSPELS
M	Ezek. 37.15–28	Heb. 7. 1–10	John 20. 1–10
T	38.10–23	7.11–28	20.11–23
W	39.21–29	8	20.24–31
T	43. 1– 9	9 1–14	21. 1–14
F	44. 4– 8	9.15–28	21.15–19
S	47. 1–12	10. 1–18	21.20–25

Pentecost 7

	O.T.	EPISTLES	GOSPELS
M	Dan. 1	Heb. 10.19–39	Matt. 1.18–25
T	2. 1–12	11. 1–12	2. 1–23
W	2.13–24	11.13–22	3. 1–17
T	2.25–46	11.23–40	4. 1–11
F	3. 1–18	12. 1–11	4.12–25
S	3.19–30	12.12–29	5. 1–12

Pentecost 8

	O.T.	EPISTLES	GOSPELS
M	Dan. 4. 1–18	Heb. 13. 1– 6	Matt. 5.13–20
T	4.19–37	13. 7–16	5.21–26
W	5. 1–12	13.17–25	5.27–37
T	5.13–30	1 Pet. 1. 1–12	5.38–48
F	6. 1–14	1.13–25	6. 1–15
S	6.15–28	2. 1–10	6.16–34

	O.T.	EPISTLES	GOSPELS

Pentecost 9

	O.T.		EPISTLES		GOSPELS	
M	Dan.	8. 1–14	1 Pet.	2.11–15	Matt.	7. 1–12
T		8.15–27		3. 1–12		7.13–29
W		9. 1–19		3.13–22		8. 1–13
T		9.20–27		4. 1–11		8.14–22
F		10. 1–14		4.12–19		8.23–34
S		12		5		9. 1– 8

Pentecost 10

	O.T.		EPISTLES		GOSPELS	
M	Ezra	1	Acts	1. 1–14	Matt.	9. 9–17
T		3		1.15–26		9.18–26
W		7.11–28		2. 1–13		9.27–38
T		8.15–32		2.14–36		10. 1– 8
F	Neh.	1		2.37–47		10. 9–15
S		2		3. 1–10		10.16–23

Pentecost 11

	O.T.		EPISTLES		GOSPELS	
M	Neh.	4. 1–14	Acts	3.11—4.4	Matt.	10.24–33
T		4.15–23		4. 5–22		10.34—11.1
W		6. 1–15		4.23–31		11. 2– 6
T		8. 1–12		4.32—5.11		11. 7–19
F		8.13–18		5.12–26		11.20–30
S		13.15–22		5.27–42		12. 1– 8

Pentecost 12

	O.T.		EPISTLES		GOSPELS	
M	Jonah	1. 1–16	Acts	6. 1–15	Matt.	12. 9–21
T		1.17—2.10		7. 1–16		12.22–37
W		3		7.17–36		12.38–50
T		4		7.37–53		13. 1– 9
F	Hag.	1. 1–11		7.54—8.3		13.10–23
S		1.12—2.9		8. 4–25		13.24–33

Pentecost 13

	O.T.		EPISTLES		GOSPELS	
M	Zech.	1. 7–17	Acts	8.26–40	Matt.	13.34–43
T		1.18—2.13		9. 1–19a		13.44–58
W		3		9.19b–31		14. 1–12
T		4		9.32–43		14.13–21
F		5		10. 1–16		14.22–36
S		6.1–8		10.17–33		15. 1–20

	O.T.	EPISTLES	GOSPELS

Pentecost 14

M	Zech. 6. 9–15	Acts 10.34–48	Matt. 15.22–28
T	7. 1– 7	11. 1–18	15.29–39
W	7. 8–14	11.19–30	16. 1–12
T	8. 1– 8	12. 1–11	16.13–28
F	8. 9–17	12.12–25	17. 1–13
S	8.18–23	13. 1–12	17.14–27

Pentecost 15

M	Prov. 1.20–33	Acts 13.13–41	Matt. 18. 1–10
T	3.11–20	13.42—14.7	18.11–22
W	4	14. 8–23	18.23–35
T	6. 6–19	15. 1–21	19. 1–15
F	7. 6–23	15.22–35	19.16–23
S	8. 1–21	15.36—16.5	19.24–30

Pentecost 16

M	Prov. 8.22–36	Acts 16. 6–24	Matt. 20. 1–16
T	9. 1–10	16.25–40	20.17–34
W	10. 1–13	17. 1–15	21. 1–17
T	11. 1–12	17.16–34	21.18–32
F	12. 9–22	18. 1–21	21.33–46
S	13. 7–25	18.22—19.7	22. 1–14

Pentecost 17

M	Prov. 14. 1–12	Acts 19. 8–20	Matt. 22.15–33
T	14.27–35	19.21–41	22.34–46
W	15. 1–15	20. 1–16	23. 1–12
T	15.16–33	20.17–38	23.13–39
F	16.16–32	21. 1–16	24. 1–14
S	18. 9–24	21.17–26	24.15–28

Pentecost 18

	Prov.	*or* Ecclus.	Acts	Matt.
M	22. 1–12	2	21.27–39	24.29–34
T	23.15–25	4.11–28	21.40—22.21	24.35–51
W	24.19–34	4.29—6.1	22.22—23.11	25. 1–13
T	25.11–28	11. 7–28	23.12–35	25.14–30

64

	O.T.			EPISTLES	GOSPELS
	Prov.	*or*	Ecclus.	Acts	Matt.
F	26. 1–12		18. 1–13	24. 1–23	25.31–46
S	27. 6–22		28. 1–12	24.24—25.12	26. 1–13

Pentecost 19

	Prov.	*or*	Ecclus.	Acts	Matt.
M	28.12–28		29. 1–13	25.13–27	26.14–29
T	29.11–27		35. 1–11	26. 1–23	26.30–46
W	30. 1– 9		36. 1–17	26.24–32	26.47–56
T	30.15–31		44. 1–15	27. 1– 8	26.57–75
F	31.10–31		51. 1–12	27. 9–26	27. 1–10
S	Obadiah		51.13–30	27.27–44	27.11–26

Pentecost 20

	Esther	*or*	1 Macc.	Acts	Matt.
M	2. 5–18		1. 1–15	28. 1–15	27.27–37
T	2.20—3.6		1.16–40	28.16–31	27.38–44
W	3. 7—4.3		1.41–64	Jude 1–16	27.45–56
T	4. 4—5.14		2. 1–22	17–25	27.57–66
F	6. 1—7.10		2.23–48	2 John	28. 1–10
S	8		2.49–69	3 John	28.11–20

Pentecost 21

	Lev.	*or*	1 Macc.	Eph.	Luke
M	23. 1–22		3. 1–26	4. 1–16	6.20–26
T	23.23–44		3.42–60	4.17–32	6.27–38
W	25. 1–24		4. 1–25	5. 1–14	6.39–49
T	25.25–55		4.36–51	5.15–33	Matt 6. 1–13
F	26. 1–13		4.52–61	6. 1– 9	6.14–23
S	26.14–20,38–45		Pr. of Manasses	6.10–24	6.24–34

NOTES

1. If more Sundays after Christmas are needed, readings from Pentecost 21 may be used.
2. Readings from 18 December and following take priority over readings from second Sunday before Christmas.

THE CANTICLES AND HYMNS

The Group believed that there was need for variation in the canticles and eventually decided that each day should have its own proper set. Most of the canticles chosen are already well known and have played an integral part in the devotional life of the Church for centuries. Those which are new or not so well known are as follows:

1. **Tuesday evening**

Benedictus es

A canticle used in the daily office of some provinces of the Anglican Communion.

2. **Friday evening and Saturday morning**

Dignus es (from Rev. 4 and 5); and *Magna et Mirabilia (Rev. 15. 3b–4).*

These are New Testament passages which have appeared in the draft of the proposed Roman Catholic daily office.

3. **Thursday evening**

Phos Hilaron

Keble's translation of one of the earliest hymns of the Christian Church outside the New Testament.

4. **Friday morning**

Salvator Mundi

A canticle well known in Free Church worship.

5. **Saturday evening**

Easter Anthems

A canticle provided for use on Easter Day in the Book of Common Prayer. It is appropriate that it should be used on Saturday evenings; it looks forward to Sunday as the weekly commemoration of the resurrection. When the Prayer Book was being revised in 1661–2, some revisers did in fact suggest that it should be used every week.

It is suggested that people should use whatever text of these canticles is most familiar to them; they are not bound to use the versions which follow here.

MONDAY

Morning

Te Deum, parts 1 and 2

1 We praise thee, O God; we acknowledge thee to be the Lord.
2 All the earth doth worship thee, the Father everlasting.
3 To thee all angels cry aloud, the heavens and all the powers therein.
4 To thee Cherubim and Seraphim continually do cry,
5 Holy, Holy, Holy, Lord God of hosts;
6 Heaven and earth are full of the majesty of thy glory.
7 The glorious company of the apostles praise thee.
8 The goodly fellowship of the prophets praise thee.
9 The noble army of martyrs praise thee.
10 The holy Church throughout all the world doth acknowledge thee,
11 The Father, of an infinite majesty;
12 Thine honourable, true, and only Son;
13 Also the Holy Ghost, the Comforter.

14 Thou art the King of Glory, O Christ;
15 Thou art the everlasting Son of the Father.
16 When thou tookest upon thee to deliver man, thou didst not abhor the Virgin's womb.
17 When thou hadst overcome the sharpness of death, thou didst open the kingdom of heaven to all believers.
18 Thou sittest at the right hand of God, in the glory of the Father.
19 We believe that thou shalt come to be our Judge.
20 We therefore pray thee, help thy servants, whom thou hast redeemed with thy precious blood.
21 Make them to be numbered with thy saints, in glory everlasting.

Evening

Magnificat (St Luke 1. 46–55)

1 My soul doth magnify the Lord: and my spirit hath rejoiced in God my Saviour.
2 For he hath regarded: the lowliness of his hand-maiden.
3 For behold, from henceforth: all generations shall call me blessed.
4 For he that is mighty hath magnified me: and holy is his name.
5 And his mercy is on them that fear him: throughout all generations.
6 He hath showed strength with his arm; he hath scattered the proud in the imagination of their hearts.

67

7 He hath put down the mighty from their seat: and hath exalted the humble and meek.

8 He hath filled the hungry with good things: and the rich he hath sent empty away.

9 He remembering his mercy: hath helped his servant Israel;

10 As he promised to our forefathers: Abraham and his seed, for ever.

Glory be to the Father, and to the Son: and to the Holy Spirit;
As it was in the beginning, is now, and ever shall be: world without end. Amen.

TUESDAY

Morning

Benedicite, omnia opera (Shortened Form)

1 O all ye works of the Lord, bless ye the Lord: praise him, and magnify him for ever.

2 O ye angels of the Lord, bless ye the Lord: praise him, and magnify him for ever.

3 O ye children of men, bless ye the Lord: praise him, and magnify him for ever.

4 O ye people of God, bless ye the Lord: praise him, and magnify him for ever.

5 O ye priests of the Lord, bless ye the Lord: praise him, and magnify him for ever.

6 O ye servants of the Lord, bless ye the Lord: praise him, and magnify him for ever.

7 O ye spirits and souls of the righteous, bless ye the Lord: praise him, and magnify him for ever.

8 Let us bless the Father, the Son, and the Holy Spirit: let us praise him, and magnify him for ever.

9 Blessed art thou, O Lord, in the firmament of heaven: to be praised, and magnified above all for ever.

Evening

Benedictus es

1 Blessed art thou, O Lord of our fathers: praised and exalted above all for ever.

2 Blessed art thou for the Name of thy Majesty: praised and exalted above all for ever.

3 Blessed art thou in the temple of thy holiness: praised and exalted above all for ever.

4 Blessed art thou that beholdest the depths, and dwellest between the Cherubin: praised and exalted above all for ever.

5 Blessed art thou on the glorious throne of thy kingdom: praised and exalted above all for ever.

6 Blessed art thou in the firmament of heaven: praised and exalted above all for ever.

Glory be to the Father, and to the Son: and to the Holy Spirit;
As it was in the beginning, is now, and ever shall be: world without end.
Amen.

WEDNESDAY

Morning

Benedictus (St Luke 1. 68–79)

1 Blessed be the Lord God of Israel: for he hath visited, and redeemed his people;

2 And hath raised up a mighty salvation for us; in the house of his servant David;

3 As he spake by the mouth of his holy prophets: which have been since the world began;

4 That we should be saved from our enemies: and from the hands of all that hate us;

5 To perform the mercy promised to our forefathers: and to remember his holy covenant;

6 To perform the oath: which he sware to our forefather Abraham;

7 That we being delivered out of the hands of our enemies: might serve him without fear;

8 In holiness and righteousness before him: all the days of our life.

9 And thou child shalt be called the Prophet of the Highest: for thou shalt go before the face of the Lord to prepare his ways;

10 To give knowledge and salvation unto his people: for the remission of their sins,

11 Through the tender mercy of our God: whereby the day-spring from on high hath visited us;

12 To give light to them that sit in darkness, and in the shadow of death: and to guide our feet into the way of peace.

Glory be to the Father, and to the Son: and to the Holy Spirit;
As it was in the beginning, is now and ever shall be: world without end. Amen.

Evening

Nunc Dimittis (Luke 2. 29–32)

1 Lord, now lettest thou thy servant depart in peace: according to thy word,

2 For mine eyes have seen thy salvation: which thou hast prepared before the face of all people;

3 To be a light to lighten the Gentiles: and to be the glory of thy people Israel.

Glory be to the Father, and to the Son: and to the Holy Spirit;
As it was in the beginning, is now and ever shall be: world without end Amen.

THURSDAY

Morning

Gloria in excelsis

Glory be to God on high,
and in earth, good will towards men.
We praise thee, we bless thee,
we worship thee, we glorify thee,
we give thanks to thee for thy great glory,
O Lord God, heavenly King,
God the Father Almighty.

O Lord, the only-begotten Son, Jesu Christ:
O Lord God, Lamb of God, Son of the Father,
that takest away the sins of the world,
have mercy upon us.
Thou that takest away the sins of the world,
receive our prayer.
Thou that sittest at the right hand of God the Father,
have mercy upon us.

For thou only art Holy;
thou only art the Lord;
thou only, O Christ, with the Holy Ghost,
art the Most High, in the glory of God the Father. Amen.

Evening

Phos Hilaron (Anonymous, c. 3rd cent; trans. John Keble)

1 Hail gladdening Light, of his pure glory poured,
   Who is the immortal Father, heavenly, blest,
   Holiest of Holies, Jesus Christ, our Lord!

2 Now we are come to the sun's hour of rest,
   The lights of evening round us shine,
   We hymn the Father, Son, and Holy Spirit divine.

3 Worthiest art thou at all times to be sung
   With undefiled tongue,
   Son of our God, Giver of life, alone!
   Therefore in all the world thy glories, Lord, they own. Amen.

FRIDAY

Morning

Salvator Mundi (Anonymous)

1 O Saviour of the world, the Son Lord Jesus:
   Stir up thy strength and help us, we humbly beseech thee.

2 By thy cross and precious blood thou hast redeemed us:
   Save us and help us, we humbly beseech thee.

3 Thou didst save thy disciples when ready to perish:
   Hear us and save us, we humbly beseech thee.

4 Let the pitifulness of thy great mercy:
   Loose us from our sins, we humbly beseech thee.

5 Make it appear that thou art our Saviour and mighty Deliverer:
   O save us that we may praise thee, we humbly beseech thee.

6 Draw near according to thy promise from the throne of thy glory:
   Look down and hear our crying, we humbly beseech thee.

7 Come again and dwell with us, O Lord Christ Jesus:
   Abide with us for ever, we humbly beseech thee.

8 And when thou shalt appear with power and great glory:
   May we be made like unto thee in thy glorious kingdom.

9 Thanks be to thee, O Lord.
   Alleluia! Amen.

Evening

Dignus es (Revelation 4.11; 5.9, 10, 13b)

1 Worthy art thou, our Lord and God, to receive glory and honour and power,

2 For thou didst create all things, and by thy will they existed and were created.

3 Worthy art thou, O Christ, for thou wast slain, and by thy blood didst ransom men for God

4 From every tribe and tongue and people and nation, and hast made them a kingdom and priests to our God.

5 To him who sits upon the throne and to the Lamb: be blessing and honour and glory and might for ever and ever. Amen.

SATURDAY

Morning

Magna et mirabilia (Revelation 15. 3b–4)

1 Great and wonderful are thy deeds; O Lord God the Almighty!
2 Just and true are thy ways; O King of the ages!
3 Who shall not fear and glorify thy name, O Lord? For thou alone art holy.
4 All nations shall come and worship thee; For thy judgements have been revealed.

Glory be to the Father, and to the Son: and to the Holy Spirit;
As it was in the beginning, is now and ever shall be: world without end. Amen.

Evening

The Easter Anthems
(1 Corinthians 5. 7–8; Romans 6. 9–11; 1 Corinthians 15. 20–2)

1 Christ our passover is sacrificed for us: therefore let us keep the feast;
2 Not with the old leaven, nor with the leaven of malice and wickedness: but with the unleavened bread of sincerity and truth.
3 Christ being raised from the dead dieth no more: death hath no more dominion over him.
4 For in that he died, he died unto sin once: but in that he liveth, he liveth unto God.
5 Likewise reckon ye also yourselves to be dead indeed unto sin: but alive unto God through Jesus Christ our Lord.
6 Christ is risen from the dead: and become the first-fruits of them that slept.
7 For since by man came death: by man came also the resurrection of the dead.
8 For as in Adam all die: even so in Christ shall all be made alive.

Glory be to the Father, and to the Son: and to the Holy Spirit;
As it was in the beginning, is now, and ever shall be: world without end. Amen.

The following is a selection of hymns which may be used in place of the canticles.

MONDAY

Morning   Christ, whose glory fills the skies
Evening   Now thank we all our God

TUESDAY

Morning   Holy, Holy, Holy! Lord God Almighty
Evening   O Jesu, King most wonderful (Jesu, the very thought of thee, part 2)

WEDNESDAY

Morning   Praise to the Lord, the Almighty, the King of creation
Evening   Jesus shall reign where'er the sun

THURSDAY

Morning   Let all the world in every corner sing
Evening   At the name of Jesus every knee shall bow

FRIDAY

Morning   Come, let us join our cheerful songs
Evening   All hail the power of Jesus' name

SATURDAY

Morning   Rejoice! the Lord is King
Evening   Songs of praise the angels sang

SEASONAL HYMNS

Pre-Christmas	The God of Abraham praise
	All creatures of our God and King
Advent	Hark the glad sound! the Saviour comes
	O come, O come, Emmanuel
Christmas	O come, all ye faithful
	Of the Father's love begotten
Passiontide	O sacred head surrounded (sore wounded)
	The royal banners forward go

Easter	Love's redeeming work is done Ye choirs of new Jerusalem
Ascension	Hail the day that sees him rise The head that once was crowned with thorns
Pentecost	Come down, O Love divine Come, Holy Ghost, our souls inspire

THE APOSTLES' CREED

I believe in God the Father Almighty,
maker of heaven and earth:

And in Jesus Christ his only Son our Lord,
who was conceived by the Holy Ghost,
born of the Virgin Mary,
suffered under Pontius Pilate,
was crucified, dead, and buried,
he descended into hell;
the third day he rose again from the dead,
he ascended into heaven,
and sitteth on the right hand of God the Father Almighty;
from thence he shall come
to judge the quick and the dead.

I believe in the Holy Ghost;
the holy catholic Church;
the Communion of Saints;
the Forgiveness of sins;
the Resurrection of the body;
and the Life everlasting. Amen.

THE ACT OF PENITENCE

Let us confess our sins to Almighty God.

Most merciful God,
We confess that we have sinned against thee
In thought, word, and deed.
We have not loved thee with our whole heart.
We have not loved our neighbours as ourselves.
We pray thee of thy mercy
    to forgive what we have been,
    to help us to amend what we are,
    and to direct what we shall be;
That we may delight in thy will
And walk in thy ways,
Through Jesus Christ our Lord. Amen.

Either

Christ Jesus came into the world to save sinners.
Hear then, the word of grace and the assurance of pardon:
Your sins are forgiven for his sake:

Or

Almighty God have mercy upon you,
Pardon and deliver you from all your sins,
Confirm and strengthen you in all goodness,
And keep you in life eternal;
Through Jesus Christ our Lord. Amen.

THE COLLECTS

(A) COLLECTS OF THE DAY

Like many traditional forms of the Daily Office, the proposed
Office contains a Collect of the Day; and it is intended that the Collect of the Sunday should serve this purpose throughout the week,
unless some special day or occasion occurs. It is obviously appropriate that the collects should be related to the Office Lectionary;
and as this is itself related to the previously published *Calendar and
Lectionary* (a lectionary for divine service, whether or not eucharis-
tic, on Sundays and special days), these collects will also serve as a
set which can be used on Sundays and special days, with that
lectionary, where collects are needed. Because of the innovations
in that Calendar and Lectionary, no existing set will do as it stands.
But many of the existing collects in their traditional Anglican form
are of great beauty and are used in non-Anglican Churches also. We
have therefore tried to retain what we believe to be the best of them,
sometimes on their traditional days, sometimes by rearrangement.
Where we could not find any such collect that was particularly suitable to the lections, we have sought other existing collects, and we
have drawn a number from the *Book of Common Worship* of the
Church of South India and from various other sources.

The style of the collects presents a problem. Both in their Latin
form and in Cranmerian English they are of great beauty; and the
attempt to modernize them, especially by addressing God in the
second person plural, has a very disturbing effect on their structure.
We have avoided this difficulty by retaining the address to God in
the second person singular, and by revising them only very slightly.
The collects from the Book of Common Prayer are so familiar that
it seems best to use them largely unchanged or not to use them at all.
But where the collects are drawn from other sources and are thus
less familiar, we have felt free to take greater liberties with them,
often by simplifying them, but sometimes by more considerable
alterations. We have, however, on the whole kept the general style
of collects. If at some future date the whole office is put into more

modern English with the address to God in the second person plural, then the use of the collect form itself will have to be reconsidered.

9th before Christmas

Almighty God, who hast created the heavens and the earth, and hast made man in thine own image: Grant us in all thy works to perceive thy hand, and ever to praise thee for thy wisdom and love; through Jesus Christ our Lord. *C.S.I., Easter 9 (amended)*

8th before Christmas

O God, whose blessed Son was manifested that he might destroy the works of the devil, and make us thy sons and heirs of eternal life: Grant that, having this hope, we may purify ourselves even as he is pure; that we may be made like unto him in his eternal and glorious kingdom: where with thee, O Father, he is alive and reigns in the unity of the Holy Spirit, one God, world without end. *B.C.P., Epiphany 6 (amended)*

7th before Christmas

Almighty and everlasting God, who dost govern all things in heaven and earth: Mercifully hear the supplications of thy people, and grant us thy peace all the days of our life; through Jesus Christ our Lord.
B.C.P., Epiphany 2

6th before Christmas

O God, who didst promise to faithful Abraham that in him all the families of the earth would be blessed: Grant us a firm faith, that in us thy promises may be fulfilled; through Jesus Christ our Lord.
C.S.I., Pentecost 4 (amended)

5th before Christmas

O God the Redeemer, who didst send thy servant Moses to lead thy people out of slavery and affliction: Rescue us from enslavement to sin and bring us to the country which thou hast prepared for us; through Jesus Christ our Lord. *C.S.I., Pentecost 22 (amended)*

4th before Christmas. Advent 1

Almighty God, give us grace that we may cast away the works of darkness, and put upon us the armour of light, now in the time of this mortal life, in which thy Son Jesus Christ came to visit us in great humility: that in the last day, when he shall come again in his glorious Majesty to judge both the quick and the dead, we may rise to the life immortal; through him who is alive and reigns with thee and the Holy Spirit, now and for ever. *B.C.P., Advent 1 (amended)*

3rd before Christmas. Advent 2

Blessed Lord, who has caused all holy Scriptures to be written for our learning: Grant that we may in such wise hear them, read, mark, learn, and inwardly digest them, that by patience, and comfort of thy holy Word, we may embrace, and ever hold fast the blessed hope of everlasting life, which thou hast given us in our Saviour Jesus Christ. *B.C.P., Advent 2*

2nd before Christmas. Advent 3

O Lord Jesu Christ, who at thy first coming didst send thy messenger to prepare thy way before thee: Grant that the ministers and stewards of thy mysteries may likewise so prepare and make ready thy way, by turning the hearts of the disobedient to the wisdom of the just, that at thy second coming to judge the world we may be found an acceptable people in thy sight, who livest and reignest with the Father and the Holy Spirit, ever one God, world without end. *B.C.P., Advent 3*

1st before Christmas. Advent 4

O God, who didst choose the blessed Virgin Mary to become the mother of our Saviour: Grant that we, having in remembrance her exceeding faith and love, may in all things seek to do thy will, and evermore rejoice in thy salvation; through Jesus Christ thy Son, our only Mediator and Advocate. *Colquhoun 556 (amended)*

Christmas Day

1. O God, who hast made this most holy night to shine with the brightness of thy one true Light: Grant that we who have known the revelation of his light on earth may attain the fulness of his joy in heaven; through Jesus Christ our Lord. *Roman Missal (newly translated)*

2. Almighty God, who hast given us thy only-begotten Son to take our nature upon him, and as at this time to be born of a pure Virgin: Grant that we being regenerate, and made thy children by adoption and grace, may daily be renewed by thy Holy Spirit; through the same our Lord Jesus Christ, who is alive and reigns with thee and the same Spirit, ever one God, world without end. *B.C.P., Christmas Day (amended)*

1st after Christmas

O God, who by the shining of a star didst lead the wise men to the worship of thy Son: Guide by thy light the nations of the earth that the world may be filled with thy glory; through Jesus Christ our Lord.

C.S.I., Christmas 2 (amended)

2nd after Christmas

O God, whose blessed Son came into the world to do thy will: Grant that we may ever have the pattern of his holy life before our eyes and find it our delight to do thy will and finish thy work; through the same Jesus Christ our Lord. *Colquhoun 321 (amended)*

3rd after Christmas

O Lord Jesus Christ, who didst humble thyself to take the baptism of sinful men, and wast there declared to be the Son of God: Grant that we who have been baptized in thee may rejoice to be the sons of God, and servants of all; for thy name's sake, who with the Father and the Holy Spirit art one God for ever and ever. *C.S.I., Christmas 4 (amended)*

4th after Christmas

Remember, O Lord, what thou hast wrought in us and not what we deserve; and as thou hast called us to thy service, make us worthy of our calling; through Jesus Christ our Lord.
1928 Prayer Book, Occasional Prayers

5th after Christmas

Almighty God, who in Christ makest all things new: Transform the poverty of our nature into the riches of thy grace, that by the renewal of our lives thy glory may be revealed; through Jesus Christ our Lord.
C.S.I., Christmas 6 (amended)

6th after Christmas

Grant, we beseech thee, merciful Lord, to thy faithful people pardon and peace, that they may be cleansed from all their sins, and serve thee with a quiet mind; through Jesus Christ our Lord. *B.C.P., Trinity 21*

9th before Easter

O Lord, we beseech thee mercifully to receive the prayers of thy people which call upon thee; and grant that they may both perceive and know what things they ought to do, and also may have grace and power faithfully to fulfil the same; through Jesus Christ our Lord.
B.C.P., Epiphany 1

8th before Easter

Almighty and most merciful God, of thy bountiful goodness keep us, we beseech thee, from all things that may hurt us; that we, being ready both in body and soul, may cheerfully accomplish those things that thou wouldest have done; through Jesus Christ our Lord.
B.C.P., Trinity 20 (amended)

7th before Easter

Almighty and everlasting God, mercifully look upon our infirmities, and in all our dangers and necessities stretch forth thy right hand to help and defend us; through Jesus Christ our Lord. *B.C.P., Epiphany 3*

Ash Wednesday

Almighty and everlasting God, who hatest nothing that thou hast made, and dost forgive the sins of all them that are penitent: Create and make in us new and contrite hearts, that we worthily lamenting our sins, and acknowledging our wretchedness, may obtain of thee, the God of all mercy, perfect remission and forgiveness; through Jesus Christ our Lord. *B.C.P., Ash Wednesday*

6th before Easter. Lent 1

Lord Jesus Christ, who wast in all points tempted as we are: Strengthen us, we pray thee, in our manifold temptations; and as thou knowest our weaknesses, so may we know thee mighty to save; who with the Father and the Holy Spirit art one God for ever and ever.

Colquhoun 1301 (amended)

5th before Easter. Lent 2

Lord, we beseech thee, grant thy people grace to withstand the temptations of the world, the flesh, and the devil, and with pure hearts and minds to follow thee the only God; through Jesus Christ our Lord.

B.C.P., Trinity 18

4th before Easter. Lent 3

Almighty God, whose most dear Son went not up to joy but first he suffered pain, and entered not into glory before he was crucified: Mercifully grant that we, walking in the way of the cross, may find it none other than the way of life and peace; through the same thy Son Jesus Christ our Lord. *American Prayer Book, Monday before Easter*

3rd before Easter. Lent 4

O God, who before the passion of thine only-begotten Son didst reveal his glory upon the holy mount: Grant unto us thy servants, that in faith beholding the light of his countenance, we may be strengthened to bear the cross, and be changed into his likeness from glory to glory; through the same Jesus Christ our Lord. *1928 Prayer Book, The Transfiguration*

2nd before Easter. Lent 5. Passion Sunday

O God, who by the cross and passion of thy Son Jesus Christ didst save and deliver mankind: Grant that by steadfast faith in his sacrifice we may triumph in the power of his victory; through the same Jesus Christ our Lord. *Scottish Prayer Book, Passiontide Collects (amended)*

1st before Easter. Palm Sunday

Almighty and everlasting God, who, of thy tender love towards mankind, hast sent thy Son, our Saviour Jesus Christ, to take upon him our flesh, and to suffer death upon the cross, that all mankind should follow the example of his great humility: Mercifully grant, that we may both follow the example of his patience, and also be made partakers of his resurrection; through the same Jesus Christ our Lord. *B.C.P., Palm Sunday*

Good Friday

Almighty God, we beseech thee graciously to behold this thy family, for which our Lord Jesus Christ was contented to be betrayed, and given up into the hands of wicked men, and to suffer death upon the cross; who now is alive and reigns with thee and the Holy Spirit, ever one God, world without end. *B.C.P., Good Friday (amended)*

Easter Day

O God, who for our redemption didst give thine only-begotten Son to the death of the cross, and by his glorious resurrection hast delivered us from the power of our enemy: Grant us so to die daily unto sin, that we may evermore live with him in the joy of his resurrection; through the same Jesus Christ our Lord. *1928 Prayer Book, Easter Day additional collect*

1st after Easter

Almighty God, who hast given unto us the true bread that comes down from heaven, even thy Son Jesus Christ: Grant that we may be fed by him who gives life to the world, that we may abide in him and he in us; who is alive and reigns with thee and the Holy Spirit, one God for ever and ever. *Macnutt, The Prayer Manual 398 (amended)*

2nd after Easter

Be thou thyself, O Lord, we pray thee, the Shepherd of thy people: that we who are protected by thy care may be strengthened by thy risen presence; for thy Name's sake. *Colquhoun 324 (amended)*

3rd after Easter

Merciful God, who hast made thy Son Jesus Christ to be the resurrection and life of all the faithful: Raise us, we pray thee, from the death of sin unto the life of righteousness, that we may seek those things which are above; where he is alive and reigns with thee and the Holy Spirit, one God, for ever and ever. *Anglican Series 2 Burial Service (amended)*

83

4th after Easter

Almighty God, whom truly to know is everlasting life: Grant us so perfectly to know thy Son Jesus Christ to be the way, the truth, and the life; that, following the steps of thy holy apostles, we may steadfastly walk in the way that leadeth to eternal life; through the same thy Son Jesus Christ our Lord.   *B.C.P., St Philip and St James (amended)*

5th after Easter

Almighty and everlasting God, who art always more ready to hear than we to pray, and art wont to give more than either we desire, or deserve: Pour down upon us the abundance of thy mercy; forgiving us those things whereof our conscience is afraid, and giving us those things which we are not worthy to ask, but through the merits and meditation of Jesus Christ, thy Son, our Lord.   *B.C.P., Trinity 12*

Ascension Day

Grant, we beseech thee, Almighty God, that like as we do believe thy only-begotten Son our Lord Jesus Christ to have ascended into the heavens; so we may also in heart and mind thither ascend, and with him continually dwell, who is alive and reigns with thee and the Holy Spirit, one God, world without end.   *B.C.P., Ascension (amended)*

6th after Easter

Almighty God, whose Son our Saviour Jesus Christ ascended far above all heavens that he might fill all things: Grant that thy Church on earth may be filled with his presence and that he may remain with us always, even unto the end of the world, through the same Jesus Christ our Lord.
                    Scottish Prayer Book, Postcommunion

Pentecost

God, who as at this time didst teach the hearts of thy faithful people, by the sending to them the light of thy Holy Spirit: Grant us by the same Spirit to have a right judgement in all things, and evermore to rejoice in his holy comfort; through the merits of Christ Jesus our Saviour, who is alive, and reigns with thee, in the unity of the same Spirit, one God, world without end.   *B.C.P., Whitsunday (amended)*

1st after Pentecost, Trinity Sunday

Almighty and everlasting God, who hast revealed thyself as Father, Son, and Holy Spirit, and dost ever live and reign in the perfect unity of love: Grant that we may always hold firmly and joyfully to this faith, and, living n praise of thy divine majesty, may finally be one in thee; who art three Persons in one God, world without end.   *C.S.I., Pentecost 1*

2nd after Pentecost

Almighty and everlasting God, by whose Spirit the whole body of the Church is governed and sanctified: Receive our supplications and prayers, which we offer before thee for all estates of men in thy holy Church, that every member of the same, in his vocation and ministry, may truly and godly serve thee; through our Lord and Saviour Jesus Christ.   *B.C.P., Good Friday* 2

3rd after Pentecost

Grant, O Lord, that as we are baptized into the death of thy Son our Saviour Jesus Christ, so by continual mortifying our corrupt affections we may be buried with him; and that through the grave, and gate of death, we may pass to our joyful resurrection; for his merits, who died, and was buried, and rose again for us, thy Son Jesus Christ our Lord.

B.C.P., Easter Even

4th after Pentecost

Almighty God, who hast given thine only Son to be unto us both a sacrifice for sin, and also an ensample of godly life: Give us grace that we may always most thankfully receive that his inestimable benefit, and also daily endeavour ourselves to follow the blessed steps of his most holy life; through the same Jesus Christ our Lord.   *B.C.P., Easter 2*

5th after Pentecost

Almighty God, who showest to them that be in error the light of thy truth, to the intent that they may return into the way of righteousness: Grant unto all them that are admitted into the fellowship of Christ's religion, that they may eschew those things that are contrary to their profession, and follow all such things as are agreeable to the same; through our Lord Jesus Christ.   *B.C.P., Easter 3*

6th after Pentecost

O God, forasmuch as without thee we are not able to please thee: Mercifully grant, that thy Holy Spirit may in all things direct and rule our hearts; through Jesus Christ our Lord.   *B.C.P., Trinity 19*

7th after Pentecost

O Lord, who hast taught us that all our doings without charity are nothing worth: Send thy Holy Spirit, and pour into our hearts that most excellent gift of charity, the very bond of peace and of all virtues, without which whosoever liveth is counted dead before thee: Grant this for thine only Son Jesus Christ's sake.   *B.C.P., Quinquagesima (amended)*

8th after Pentecost

Almighty God, who didst send thy Spirit to abide in thy Church unto the end: Mercifully grant that we may receive the gifts of his grace and bring forth the fruit of the Spirit; through Jesus Christ our Lord.

Scottish Prayer Book, Whitsun Postcommunion Collect (amended)

9th after Pentecost

Almighty God, who seest that we have no power of ourselves to help ourselves: Keep us both outwardly in our bodies, and inwardly in our souls; that we may be defended from all adversities which may happen to the body, and from all evil thoughts which may assault and hurt the soul; through Jesus Christ our Lord. *B.P.C., Lent 2*

10th after Pentecost

O Lord, from whom all good things do come: Grant to us thy humble servants, that by the holy inspiration we may think those things that be good, and by thy merciful guiding may perform the same; through Jesus Christ our Lord. *B.C.P., Easter 5 (amended)*

11th after Pentecost

O Lord, who hast taught us that whatever is done to the least of thy brethren is done to thee: Make us ever willing to minister to the needs of others; to thy praise and glory, who with the Father and the Holy Spirit art God over all, blessed for ever. *St Augustine (amended)*

12th after Pentecost

Almighty and everlasting God, who didst give to thine apostles grace truly to believe and to preach thy Word: Grant, we pray thee, to thy Church to love that Word which they believed, and both to preach and receive the same; through Jesus Christ our Lord.

B.C.P., St Bartholomew (amended)

13th after Pentecost

Lord God, whose blessed Son, our Saviour, gave his back to the smiters and hid not his face from shame: Grant us to accept the sufferings of the present time, in full assurance of the glory that shall be revealed; through the same thy Son Jesus Christ our Lord.

American Prayer Book, Tuesday Before Easter (amended)

14th after Pentecost

O God, who hast taught us to keep all thy commandments by loving thee and our neighbour: Grant us the spirit of grace and peace, that we may be devoted to thee with our whole heart and united to each other with a pure will; through Jesus Christ our Lord.

A Book of Public Worship (*amended*)

15th after Pentecost

Keep, we beseech thee, O Lord, thy Church with thy perpetual mercy; and, because the frailty of man without thee cannot but fall, keep us ever by thy help from all things hurtful, and lead us to all things profitable to our salvation; through Jesus Christ our Lord.   B.C.P., *Trinity* 15

16th after Pentecost

Grant, O Lord, we beseech thee, that the course of this world may be so peaceably ordered by thy governance, that thy Church may joyfully serve thee in all godly quietness; through Jesus Christ our Lord.

B.C.P., *Trinity* 5

17th after Pentecost

Lord of all power and might, who art the author and giver of all good things: Graft in our hearts the love of thy Name, increase in us true religion, nourish us with all goodness, and of thy great mercy keep us in the same; through Jesus Christ our Lord.   B.C.P., *Trinity* 7

18th after Pentecost

O God, who hast willed to restore all things in thy beloved Son, the king of all: Grant that the families of the nations, divided and rent asunder by the wounds of sin, may be subject to his most gentle rule; who is alive and reigns with thee in the unity of the Holy Spirit, one God, world without end.

19th after Pentecost

Almighty God, who alone canst order the unruly wills and affections of sinful men: Grant unto thy people, that they may love the thing which thou commandest, and desire that which thou dost promise; that so, among the sundry and manifold changes of the world, our hearts may surely there be fixed, where true joys are to be found; through Jesus Christ our Lord.   B.C.P., *Easter* 4

20th after Pentecost

O God, who hast prepared for them that love thee such good things as pass man's understanding: Pour into our hearts such love toward thee, that we, loving thee above all things, may obtain thy promises, which exceed all that we can desire; through Jesus Christ our Lord.

B C.P., *Trinity* 6

21st after Pentecost

O God, the protector of all that trust in thee, without whom nothing is strong, nothing is holy: Increase and multiply upon us thy mercy; that, thou being our ruler and guide, we may so pass through things temporal, that we finally lose not the things eternal: Grant this, heavenly Father, for the sake of Jesus Christ, thy Son, our Lord.

B.C.P., Trinity 4 (amended)

Extra Sundays after Christmas

1. Grant to us, Lord, we pray thee, the spirit to think and do always such things as be rightful; that we, who cannot do any thing that is good without thee, may by thee be enabled to live according to thy will; through Jesus Christ our Lord. *B.C.P., Trinity 9 (amended)*

2. O God, the strength of them that put their trust in thee, mercifully accept our prayers; and because through the weakness of our mortal nature we can do no good thing without thee, grant us the help of thy grace, that in keeping of thy commandments we may please thee, both in will and deed; through Jesus Christ our Lord. *B.C.P., Trinity 1*

Extra Sundays after Pentecost

1. Lord, we beseech thee to keep thy household the Church in continual godliness; that through thy protection it may be free from all adversities, and devoutly given to serve thee in good works, to the glory of thy name; through Jesus Christ our Lord. *B.C.P., Trinity 22*

2. Stir up, we beseech thee, O Lord, the wills of thy faithful people; that they, plenteously bringing forth the fruit of good works, may of thee be plenteously rewarded; through Jesus Christ our Lord.

B.C.P., Trinity 25, next before Advent

(B) MORNING AND EVENING COLLECTS

Both in the morning and evening office we have provided a fixed prayer, suited to the time of the day. The morning collect is a new composition, emphasizing that creation and redemption are the basic facts to which we should respond in our daily lives. In order to do this we ask for the help and guidance of the Holy Spirit. The evening collect is an ancient one found in the Gelasian Sacramentary, and which was the invariable collect for Compline in the Sarum Breviary. It was translated into English, and in the Book of Common Prayer is the third collect at Evening Prayer, "For aid against all perils". Its simple beauty and appropriateness have commended it also to many Christians outside the Anglican and Roman Catholic Churches.

Morning

Eternal God and Father, by whose power we are created and by whose love we are redeemed: Guide and strengthen us by thy Spirit, that we may give ourselves to thy service, and live this day in love to one another and to thee; through Jesus Christ our Lord.

Evening

Lighten our darkness, we beseech thee, O Lord; and by thy great mercy defend us from all perils and dangers of this night; for the love of thy only Son, our Saviour, Jesus Christ.

THE INTERCESSIONS AND THANKSGIVINGS

The modernizing of the language of prayer remains a matter of debate; but the shift from traditional usage is gathering increasing momentum. Within the Office itself we have—at least for the moment—retained traditional language, mainly for the purposes of uniformity. The Old Testament of the New English Bible has not yet appeared, and the Revised Standard Version—which is used in all traditions—has traditional language; so has the Revised Psalter, and so has most of our hymnody. We feel, however, that in the Intercessions and Thanksgivings, which are outside the Office proper, a break with traditional language is both permissible and desirable.

The threefold structure of the Intercessions and Thanksgivings is the same and should be noted.

1. The opening address to God, which is expanded by reference to the particular facet of revelation in Christ which is appropriate. The progression through the week is:

MONDAY	Creation in Christ
TUESDAY	The Life of Christ
WEDNESDAY	The Cross of Christ
THURSDAY	The Resurrection of Christ
FRIDAY	The Priestly Ministry of Christ
SATURDAY	The Consummation in Christ

2. The content of the Intercessions and Thanksgivings. In the Intercessions there are six subjects for each day of the week; but it is not envisaged that all six subjects should necessarily be used every day. In the Thanksgivings there are three groups of subjects for each day, the first group often concentrating on the elaboration of the christological reference in the opening address.

3. The conclusion of petition or ascription.

The themes, which should be taken only as rough short-hand guides to the thrust and concern of the prayers, are as follows:

	Intercessions	*Thanksgivings*
MONDAY	The World	Creation and Providence
TUESDAY	Society	Revelation and Human Knowledge
WEDNESDAY	Personal Relationships	Reconciliation and Human Relationships
THURSDAY	The Church	The Divine Society: the Church
FRIDAY	The Suffering	All that meets human need
SATURDAY	The Sick and Departed	The Fulfilment of the Divine Purpose

MONDAY

Creation in Christ: Creation and Providence

1 Almighty God,
Maker of all things and Father of all men,
You have shown us in Christ the purpose of your creation and called us
to responsible service in the world.

2 *Intercession*

We pray for THE WORLD

all nations . . .
our own country . . .
those in authority . . .
the peace of the world . . .
racial harmony . . .
integration . . .

3 *Thanksgiving*

We give thanks
for the order of created things
the resources of the earth
the gift of human life . . .
for the continuing work of creation
man's share in it
creative vision and inventive skill . . .
for your faithfulness to man in patience and in love
every human response of obedience and humble achievement . . .

4 May we delight in your purpose, and
work to bring all things to their true end;
Through Jesus Christ our Lord. Amen.

TUESDAY

The Incarnate Life of Christ:
Revelation and Human Knowledge

1 God our Father
   You gave your Son, Jesus Christ
       to share our life on earth,
       to grow in wisdom,
       to toil with his hands, and
       to make known the ways of your kingdom.

2 *Intercession*

   We pray for SOCIETY

       those who work . . .
       the unemployed . . .
       those in education . . .
       those in research . . .
       those in communication . . .
       those who maintain the life of the community . . .

3 *Thanksgiving*

   We give thanks
       for his revelation of yourself
           his care for people
           his joy in obedience . . .
       for the value he gave to human labour
           the strength he promised us for service
           the call to follow in his way . . .
       for all opportunities of work and of leisure
           all truth that we have learned
           all discoveries that man has made . . .

4 Give us growing reverence for the truth, and such wisdom in the use of
       knowledge,
   That your kingdom may be advanced, and your name glorified;
   Through Jesus Christ our Lord. Amen.

WEDNESDAY

The Cross of Christ: Reconciliation and Human Relationships

1 Holy Father,
  You have reconciled us to yourself in Christ;
  By your Spirit
  You enable us to live as your children.

2 *Intercession*

  We pray for PERSONAL RELATIONSHIPS

>   the home and family life . . .
>   children deprived of home . . .
>   friends and relations . . .
>   neighbours . . .
>   relationships in daily life and work . . .
>   those who are estranged . . .

3 *Thanksgiving*

  We give thanks
>   for the obedience of Christ fulfilled in the cross
>   his bearing of the sin of the world
>   his victory over evil and death . . .
>   for the joy of human love and friendship
>   the lives to which our own are bound
>   the gift of peace with you and each other . . .
>   for the communities in whose life we share
>   all relationships in which reconciliation may be known . . .

4 Help us to share in the obedience of your Son,
  That we may love and serve one another in peace;
  Through the same Jesus Christ our Lord,
  Who in the unity of the Spirit is one with you for ever. Amen.

THURSDAY

The Resurrection of Christ: The Divine Society, the Church

1 Eternal God,
   You have raised Jesus Christ from the dead and given him glory,
   And through him called your Church into being,
   That your people might know you, and
   That they might make your Name known.

2 *Intercession*

   We pray for THE CHURCH

   > the Church, universal and local . . .
   > the unity of the Church . . .
   > the ministries of the Church . . .
   > the mission of the Church . . .
   > the renewal of the Church . . .
   > all Christians in this place . . .

3 *Thanksgiving*

   We give thanks
   > for the apostolic Gospel committed to your Church
   > > the continuing presence and power of your Spirit
   > > the ministry of Word, Sacrament, and Prayer . . .
   > for the divine mission in which we are called to share
   > > the will to unity and its fruit in common action
   > > the faithful witness of those who are true to Christ . . .
   > for all works of Christian compassion
   > > every service that proclaims your love . . .

4 In peace and unity
   may your people offer the unfailing sacrifice of praise,
   and make your glory known;
   Through Jesus Christ our Lord. Amen.

FRIDAY

The Priestly Ministry of Christ: All that meets Human Need

1 Gracious God and Father,
  You have given us in Christ a merciful Saviour,
  Who ever presents to you the world in all its need.

2 *Intercession*

We pray for THE SUFFERING

> the hungry . . .
> the refugees . . .
> the prisoners . . .
> the persecuted . . .
> agents of sin and suffering . . .
> ministries of care and relief. . . .

3 *Thanksgiving*

We give thanks

> for the cross of Christ at the heart of creation
>> the presence of Christ in our weakness and strength
>> the power of Christ to transform our suffering . . .
> for all ministries of healing
>> all agencies of relief
>> all that sets men free from pain, fear, and distress . . .
> for the assurance that your mercy knows no limit
>> the privilege of sharing your work of renewal through prayer . . .

4 In darkness and in light,
  In trouble and in joy,
  Help us to trust your love,
      to serve your purpose, and
      to praise your name;
  Through Jesus Christ our Lord. Amen.

SATURDAY

Consummation in Christ: The Fulfilment of the Divine Purpose

1 Eternal God,
You have declared in Christ
The completion of all your purpose of love.

2 *Intercession*

We pray for THE SICK AND THE DEPARTED

the tempted and despairing . . .
the sick and handicapped . . .
the aged . . .
the ministries of care and healing . . .
those who mourn . . .
the departed . . .

3 *Thanksgiving*

We give thanks
for the triumphs of the gospel that herald your salvation
the signs of renewal that declare the coming of your kingdom
the human lives that reveal your work of grace . . .
for the unceasing praise of the company of heaven
the promise to those who mourn that all tears shall be wiped
away
the pledge of death destroyed and victory won . . .
for our foretaste of eternal life through baptism and eucharist
our hope in the Spirit
the communion of saints . . .

4 May we live by faith, walk in hope, and be renewed in love,
Until the world reflects your glory
And you are all in all.
Even so, come Lord Jesus. Amen.

THE SHORTENED FORM OF
THE DAILY OFFICE

The Group clearly regards the full Daily Office, both Morning and Evening, as the norm. They recognize, however, that in certain circumstances—more particularly in the case of lay people—some abbreviation may be necessary. A single shortened form of the Office is therefore provided. It is important, however, that those who find it necessary to use the shortened form should also feel that they have still shared in the daily round of the Church's prayer. Obviously they will read less of the Psalter each day than those who use the full Office; and they will read only one or two lessons instead of three. But what they read will always be a part of what is read by those who use the Office in full.

1. THE STRUCTURE

Sentence or Versicles and Responses.

Psalm.

One or two lessons.

Silence.

Canticle or Hymn.

Act of Penitence.

The Lord's Prayer.

Collect of the Day.

If desired, the Office may be followed by Intercessions and/or Thanksgivings.

2. THE PSALMS

For the first thirteen weeks the psalms appointed for the morning should be read, for the second thirteen weeks those appointed for the evening. The entire Psalter will therefore be read twice instead of four times a year. Since the shortened office may be read at any time of the day, and may often be read at midday, the fact that some psalms are more suitable for use in the morning and others in the evening becomes immaterial. Reading the Psalter in this way will sometimes mean beginning in the middle of a psalm. In general this will be found to create no serious difficulty—the meaning of just part of a psalm will be clear. The one exception is on Friday of Week 7, when Psalm 73 would begin somewhat awkwardly at verse 16. It is therefore suggested that the whole of the psalm might be read each time the shortened form of the Office is used.

3. LESSONS

The simplest scheme for reading a single lesson would be to read through one list, Old Testament or Epistles or Gospels, each year over six years. The disadvantage of this is that reading is then restricted to one part of the Bible for a whole year. We therefore recommend the following scheme:

Year	9th before Christmas to 31 December	Christmas 1 to the end of Holy Week	Easter to the end of the year
1.	First Year OT	First Year Epistles	First Year Gospels
2.	Second Year OT	Second Year Epistles	Second Year Gospels
3.	First Year Epistles	First Year Gospels	First Year OT
4.	Second Year Epistles	Second Year Gospels	Second Year OT
5.	First Year Gospels	First Year OT	First Year Epistles
6.	Second Year Gospels	Second Year OT	Second Year Epistles

If two lessons are read, one from the Old Testament and one from the New, the lectionary can be completed in four years. The Old Testament lessons will be read as in the full Office, i.e., in Year 1 the First Year series, in Year 2 the Second Year series, in Year 3 the First Year series, and in Year 4 the Second Year series. The New Testament should be read as follows:

Year	9th before Christmas to 31 December	Christmas 1 to the end of Holy Week	Easter to the end of the year
1.	First Year Epistles	First Year Gospels	First Year Epistles
2.	Second Year Gospels	Second Year Epistles	Second Year Gospels
3.	First Year Gospels	First Year Epistles	First Year Gospels
4.	Second Year Epistles	Second Year Gospels	Second Year Epistles

4. CANTICLES AND HYMNS

Either Morning or Evening Canticles and Hymns may be used, whichever may be found to be most appropriate.

GENERAL NOTES

1. The Calendar observed in the Daily Office is that provided by the Joint Liturgical Group in their Report *The Calendar and Lectionary*, edited by Ronald C. D. Jasper (O.U.P., 7s 6d.).

2. The Daily Office provided is for week-day use only. At the moment it is envisaged that churches will use their normal services on Sundays.

3. The provision here is simply for the Temporale (or Calendar of Time). No proposals are made for Saints' Days, while arrangements for Holy Week will be considered separately in a further Report.

4. Biblical references are normally those of the Revised Standard Version; but other versions of the Bible may be used.